Driven, highly suc[illegible] for emotional openness. Simon is a rare exception. He opens up and shares how it has really been to create and run a world-class business. It is rare to deliver inspiration, and keep the magic alive through many successes and failures, over twenty-five years. His expertise and his honesty will inform and inspire you to keep moving beyond your perceived limits.

NICK WILLIAMS, inspired leadership guide and best-selling author of seventeen books including *The Work We Were Born To Do*

"Simon's deep knowledge and cunning insight shared in this book have allowed me and my community to take advantage of market opportunities we never thought existed before knowing him."

KEN RUTKOWSKI founder of METal International

"This incredible books sits at the intersection of enjoyable and educational. Simon Leslie has done an excellent job of capturing and sharing key sales and business principles that have helped him to build a phenomenal business and thrive during the incredible economic and political highs and lows of the last few decades. If you are in sales, in business or simply want to live a really interesting and fulfilling life, start now on page one."

ERIC EDMEADES founder of WildFit and author of *One Talk Away*

"A great romp through the world and life of Simon Leslie. Valuable and honest lessons in life and business that apply to anyone in sales. Equally valuable to someone starting or scaling a business."

STEVE CLARKE author, speaker and serial entrepreneur

"Simon Leslie is a man who definitely knows about life and business. As an entrepreneur, he has set himself apart in the world of business. His new book is full of wit, wisdom and principles that will take your life and business to the next level."

TIM STOREY author, speaker and life coach

First edition: July 2019

ISBN: 978-1-9161051-0-2

Cover design by Zeljka Kojic

Editing by MakeMeASuccess – Kirsten Rees

Nofinsales.com

THERE IS NO F IN SALES

A book about selling
in <u>every</u> market condition

SIMON LESLIE

CONTENTS

ACKNOWLEDGEMENTS

I WANT TO SAY THANK YOU to all the people who have helped on my journey, from the teachers who didn't believe in me, to my team who did. To the guys who did me wrong and to those who put me right. To those who tried to break me and those who put me back together, there are too many of you to thank and mention by name but I know you know who you are and which category you fall into.

To the four boys and one girl I do this all for, I love and thank you. And, of course, to my parents without whom none of this would have happened.

The only satisfactory aim in life is to reach an unattainable goal. – Simon Leslie

This book was written because I want it to help people deal with the demons that hold them back. So much so, that every penny of profit will be split between two very worthwhile causes: the first is the plight of the homeless, a 20th-century disease that urgently needs fixing. We need this sorted far more than we need self-driving cars. The second is depression, a disease that has taken over as one of the world's major killers and very much affected me and my family.

So, thanks for buying. If nothing else, you are making a worthwhile donation.

We all have choices, so I appreciate you making the choice to read or listen to this book. There are a lot of good books out there and I thank you for choosing to share my adventure with me.

The profits will be shared between Young Minds (*youngminds.org.uk*) and Centrepoint (*centrepoint.org.uk*). Both very worthwhile causes.

INTRODUCTION

IF YOU'VE SOLD ANYTHING, you've heard it – nothing happens without a sale. And not just once, it's said time after time.

My life has been a series of pushing back against hearing "no". I couldn't tell you the entire story even if I wanted to, but I can share the hard lessons, the value I've earned and the hindsight I've learned over the last few decades.

By moving forward into the unknown, I learned and I prospered. Today, I oversee a team of almost two hundred salespeople, delivering a world-class product in over sixty countries around the globe. I have offices in London, Miami, New York, Los Angeles, and Singapore and I provide services in over ten languages.

Not bad for a boy from Cardiff, South Wales. Sometimes, a lack of knowledge can be your greatest advantage. This is a teachable story of how I turned my own lack of knowledge into a proven system. It has generated over a billion dollars of revenue and in the process re-invented an entire industry.

Some say it is an art. Others say it is a grind. Selling has led me on an amazing journey that has given me so much, and now I want to give back. Through this book, I will do my best to show what I learned and how it can work for you. But know this, I can give you a road map but the journey is up to you. One thing is certain, it can be done, and you can do it! Remember to stay positive, even when there is no 'F' in Sales.

PRELUDE

I AM HERE TO TELL YOU that you can learn how to face anything. For me, it started with raw passion and steadily became a system and philosophy that has changed not only my life but also the lives of those around me.

What I discovered worked for me and it will work for you. This book will help you learn how to face your challenges and give you the tools to reach your unattainable goals. This is not a self-help book but a book set out to help others.

I'm not sure if this is a story of luck, belief, hard work, or just unflappable determination. It started on the 20th June 1986, and culminates aboard a private jet to Moscow en route to watch the World Cup Final on my fiftieth birthday with four of my oldest friends.

Over the pages, I'll explain my sales philosophy and also my thinking and motivation to create one of the greatest media sales organisations on the planet. Twenty-five years ago, it was two of us in a room above a printers in Battersea, South London. Today, I motivate, coach and inspire salespeople selling travel media across the globe.

This is a story of how a kid from South Wales with no formal education, who was actually thrown out of school and college, went on to build a sales company that empowered and inspired a generation of salespeople and managed to upset a few along the way.

I will share my journey, warts and all. Attrition, complaints, lawsuits, and a lot of the stuff I found out in the process. In this book, I will share insights in how to tackle adversity and make quick decisions to get you the outcome you want.

This is not a rags to riches story, it's a story of a middle-class kid who was a little lost, confused, and, at times, depressed. A boy with an addictive personality and a desire to win.

I live with the belief that things don't need to make sense... We must never let logic and data kill our magical existence. Sometimes you need to understand that you are attempting to get things from work that just cannot be found there. Imagine living in a place that even your younger self could not have dreamed up. A place beyond your wildest imagination – that's where I live today. You are always going to have shit days, so you can either make up a reason or just accept it's a shit day. You don't need to be a victim, it's time to be your own hero.

The hardest task is moving from miserable to magical, and some clues to finding that formula are in this book. Life will start giving you all the great things it has in store for you.

When I stopped making excuses, I discovered the results.

1

CLOSE WHEN YOU OPEN

MY PHILOSOPHY IS SIMPLE: start with the end in mind, think and dream big, and act quickly. So, let's start at the end on 15th July, 2018.

It's a fresh morning as the Mercedes picks us up and drops us at Biggin Hill Airfield. Five boys: two I met at my first job in 1986; a cheeky chappie from Liverpool; and my friend, the builder, though he prefers property developer these days. Between us we all have lovely lives and families, we are all successful and generally happy.

We all share the same traits; we want to be winners. We are all middle-aged men and still feel and behave like teenage boys. We like the best things in life. It's not just about the material things but the people who need and love us. We have given our families everything they need and now it's time for us to enjoy the second half of our lives.

As the jet takes off, the Bollinger is flowing and

the singing starts with the realisation that we are flying in a private jet to Moscow and we are going to the bloody World Cup Final.

As we arrive in Moscow, the car supposed to pick us up is not there. He can't get access to the airport. After a few chats with the local airport crew he is allowed in. First panic resolved. He doesn't speak a word of English. We communicate via Google Translate and discover that he doesn't have the tickets. After a few nerve-racking moments and frantic phone calls I find out they are at the hotel.

The boys have no idea what's going on, they are pissed and excited. I remain calm but below the surface, I am panicking. What happens if there are no tickets, what happens if I have been scammed? Is this all going to go horribly wrong? As we arrive at the hotel the receptionist tells me there are no tickets – at this point, my World Cup Final dreams are about to fall apart.

I ask slowly, "An envelope was delivered this morning for Simon Leslie?" After what feels like an age, she hands me a Manila envelope with five tickets. The dream is still on. We rush and get changed and head for the stadium. We arrive at 5:55pm for a 6pm kick off. Lucky Leslie strikes again. The final is amazing, the French dominate and lift the trophy.

Ignoring the torrential rain as we leave the stadium, we go on to have the night of our lives in Moscow – vodka and champagne flowing – I remember very little.

The next morning, I wake up with a very sore head. We head for the Russian baths where we are scrubbed, rubbed, and prodded by a naked old man in an old-fashioned steam room. A few hours sightseeing and we are back on the jet home spending most of the flight asleep. As we land back in the UK, the car is waiting on the tarmac, "This is how to live life!" I remember thinking.

What a way to celebrate fifty years on the planet. Yet, only nine months earlier, I had no idea how I would pull this off and did not even have the money to pay for it.

Take F'in Action

Plan forward – write down your business plan and goals and also the reasons why you are doing it all. "To make money" is not a goal – what do you want to spend it on? Don't be afraid to think big! There are many success stories out there from people who started out just where you are now. Be flexible, nothing ever goes the way you expect it.

2

WHERE IT ALL BEGAN

WHO AM I to have any credibility to write this book? It all began when I was a spotty seventeen-year-old. I started in business very young, with little education and even less experience. That's probably why I survived. I was too stupid to worry about what could go wrong – had I stopped to think about all the things that could go awry, I probably would never have started in the first place.

I was thrown out of school, then college, and looking back, there was a reason for it. I was not built to comply. Not built to conform. Still today, I choose the 'other path' and my compliance levels can still be pretty low but now it's for the right reasons... mostly.

On the street selling life insurance door to door, now that's a baptism of fire. Swearing, doors slammed, chased by kids, adults, and dogs. However, I managed something no one had ever done before – I sold on the very first night on the job. It was a Friday night and I was supposed to be home for the family dinner. I wasn't and no one at home was happy for me.

This was my first foray into sales. I loved the buzz. The adrenalin was unbelievable. No, it was believable. We would be driven by our team leaders and dropped in some of the roughest areas of London and go from door to door peddling our wares. At the end of the night we would be picked up with a sale or two.

This repeated every day of the week. I loved it for a time, but I had always wanted to be an estate agent. No one would give me a job, so with the money I had made, I started my own estate agency with a friend. Unfortunately for us, it happened to coincide with the property crash of the Eighties. We survived longer than most gave us credit for and it was a steep learning curve in business.

From there, I started selling advertising. Within a short time, I had a magazine and fancy offices on King's Road, in the heart of London, above McDonald's. We got used to the stench of burgers and fries from below – nothing's ever perfect! I mixed with film stars and celebrities of the day. Oh where did life go so wrong? I lived the high life and that's where I met my business partner of today.

On a quiet Monday, we first met over a PR lunch, in a restaurant called Charco's. This turned out to be rather spooky because years later, I found out the company that bought us had originally been called Charcos Limited. This is only one of many weird coincidences over the years. The lunch was shocking and we laughed over burnt food, a drunk waiter, and corked wine. I still remember Michael's words at the end of the meal in true PR style, "You will give a good review, won't you?"

Today, Michael Keating and I have built a global advertising business, launched in the USA and Asia at the same time, spent thousands of hours on airplanes and hired, fired, and inspired thousands of people to be better versions of themselves.

I have sold, bought, trained, coached, and been a listening ear. I look after people with huge egos and some with little personality and confidence issues. I juggle being a dad, a husband, and a boss, and by now I'm getting reasonably good at it. If you can create a business that makes a profit, that's your step to freedom. There is nothing in life worth having that is without stress and discomfort.

Where others see failure, I see opportunity. Not because I am dense (although I may seem so from time to time), but rather because I know! There is always a way. This has become the heart of my sales DNA. I blossom when I'm allowed to be and given space to think creatively, not when I am being held back or told what to do. If this sounds like you, fear not. If you are uncomfortable in a rigid system, get out of it. If you are thinking about trying to make it on your own, go for it!

In the beginning, this attitude was my enemy. It created arrogance and I took a lot personally. Many said I would never make it but that just drove me harder. Maybe I was plain ignorant. But it was that early ignorance that saved me. Now, with success, my youthful arrogance has become quiet confidence.

Looking back over the last thirty-three years, I have survived so much, be it wars, people challenges, recessions, financial crises. In the very beginning, I did not know how to overcome any of it, I just did. In the process, I developed a set of skills and tools that still serve me today. And they will serve you.

Nothing in this book will be unbelievable to hear, but it's not normal or ordinary either. It's an adventure through success and failure, through some dark and many magical moments. Coming from a place where most days there were no F'in sales. Today, as a business we sell over a hundred million dollars of advertising each year. That's a lot of F'in sales every single day.

The problem with most salespeople is they don't

want to be salespeople. They want to give themselves fancy titles to hide the fact that they sell shit. Most are embarrassed to say they are in sales. Understand this, until something gets sold nothing happens. Accept it, embrace it, and love it until the day you love the fact that you make things happen. Otherwise, you will always be really disappointed.

Every interaction in life is a sale – with your parents, partners, and friends. The person who is the best salesperson is the person we all follow, just look at what Trump has achieved.

The world doesn't need another book on selling. This is a guide to living a meaningful life – a journey through sales jobs, sales leadership, and how to keep the winning streak going. I wholeheartedly believe success is driven by belief and this has always been my mantra. I also now believe things will either stay the same or get better but I didn't always feel that way.

After three failed businesses, one in textiles, one in property, and one in publishing, I was really on my last legs. My father told me to get a proper job, he didn't understand I just didn't want to work for anyone else. I was compelled to create my own path.

This was the last chance to succeed, I had given myself no other options. I had burned all the bridges and removed the safety net that most hold on to. I went for it hook, line, and sinker.

My previous business partner had decided to emigrate to Australia and I started working with Michael Keating, who had moved on from his restaurant PR days. It was 1994 and we were both optimistic and excited. I was – and remain – quite humble and restrained, while Michael would tell the world we were something special. The irony is, we eventually became what he described.

We had a contract with two tiny airlines, one servicing the Middle East and the other East and Southern Africa. Beirut, Uganda, Rwanda, Kenya, Jordan, and Syria – hardly the classic business destinations on which to build a business – yet it was a start and probably the most fun time of our lives.

We muddled along for a couple of years before disaster struck – we were about to completely run out of money. This is when Leslie became Lucky Leslie. We really were a week or two from the end. One day, £57,000 showed up in our account. We had no idea who had paid us, apart from the fact it had come from the German private bank Kleinwort Benson. After a week of not being recalled, I put the money to work. I secured an overdraft against it and we continued to trade. It was really this luck that allowed us to stay in business. There have been many scary moments since then but this was the pivotal moment that allowed us to stay the course.

Oddly, some four years later, the very day after we sold the business for the first time, the German bank (which had gone through three year ends and a takeover) spotted the error and asked for the money back. Someone had been looking down on us, they waited until they knew we were secure to spot their mistake. We did a good deal and paid them back. Funny how one survives in business, it's not how they map it out in the manuals.

Every one of us is on a journey. We are tourists of life, enjoy every moment, visit as many countries as you can, do good deeds. We don't know when our journey will end, so please enjoy the ride.

Take F'in Action

Go find mentors, connect with like-minded people, and find someone to stay accountable to so you keep moving forward. Instead of being critical of yourself in lacking certain skills, have confidence in what you are good at and then go seek out people who have those other skills. Don't make work your everything. Take time to make a life.

3

DO SOMETHING WITH WHAT YOU LEARN IN THIS BOOK

THIS CANNOT BE a book you read and get all excited and inspired about and then do nothing. This book should give you so much ammunition to get your career on speed. But motivation is like a warm bath, it doesn't last long. You need to take massive action and commit to doing something and getting rid of the bad habits.

As you arrived in the world, did the doctor tell your parents, "Here you go, here is your baby, they are exactly the same as the other five babies I delivered today"? Of course not. You were the most special human in the whole world on that day and every day since. Just some days you may have allowed yourself to forget this.

There is no point in reading one word more if you are not prepared to take action. I have encountered thousands of great readers and talkers. Life is not easy, every step is a challenge, problem after problem – it's the longest hurdle race ever. Just keep reminding yourself you are at the beginning of something very special. One step in the right direction and you change your life for good.

As long as you know that, you don't get too down on your losses or too hyper on your wins, you will survive in sales. Keep your balance and make sure the quality of your problems keeps getting bigger. There are plenty of people in the ground who no longer have a problem. Life will deliver whatever it is you want as long as you do as much as you can to help others. You need to consistently show up and be present, really present.

Today, I love life. I find excitement in every challenge. I have a simple mantra: do more... and get better. Repeat.

"Boss, I can't work any harder," I hear repeatedly from my sales teams. Then figure out how you can get better. That's it. The best amongst us don't just spend their time reading and learning, they take massive action. Like great sportsmen, they train harder, they get faster and find incremental improvement in whatever they do.

Do less, achieve more. The art of achieving more is doing less and being super focused. Too many people focus on either too long a plan or they don't have one. Focus on now. Focus on the next hour and break it down into six lots of ten-minute chunks and see how few you can waste. Make the next email sensational, the next voicemail so enticing, get up and talk to someone new or find something new. Buy someone coffee and listen. Switch off your bloody mobile – phones have taken over our lives and will continue to do so. Stop showing off and lying on social media and do things only to make you happy.

One of the best bits of advice I ever received was to start your day before you look at your phone. Don't get bogged down before you need to. Get up, do your routine – whatever it is you need – have your shower, eat and hydrate yourself before you even look at the phone.

One theme I recently introduced to my teams, was imagining the time when you wished for exactly what you have right now. Be it the job, car, wife, family, or home. We don't always appreciate what we have, we don't show enough gratitude for it. We spend too much time worrying about what we don't have, or what someone else has that's better than us.

I always remind my guys that they might not be who they want to be but at least they are not who they used to be. Some of the transformations of the people who walked through our doors have been nothing short of magical.

Over the years we have helped transform salespeople's lives, freeing them from debt, student loans, and addictions. We helped people buy their first homes and even lent people the deposits. We flew families around the world to reconnect and have the best holidays together. I watched people arrive with nothing and leave with fancy cars and their foot on the property ladder.

Lots of my teams own multiple properties and send big chunks of cash home to their families. I helped them be with parents when they needed them most. My business has taken on kids straight out of school as well as guys on their last hurrah. I am so proud of the impact we have had in making so many lives better.

One story I love to share is a young girl who joined us in Singapore. She was good but thought she was better and decided to leave us. A year later she returned and has been one of our success stories.

We watched her find love, get married, and we supported her through challenges with her father's health. She had a baby and through all of this, she remained one of our best. She was stubborn but we encouraged her to get better with coaching and mentoring, and she listened and followed the process. Today, watching her multitask her parenting duties with her sales commitments makes me so proud. She is about to have her second child and continues to sell while dealing with morning sickness and she is a huge inspiration to all around her. She and her husband are planning to move soon and we are giving her the opportunity to stay with the business as they prepare to make a new life in Australia.

One day, a twenty-six-year-old Swede arrived in our London office fresh from a stint selling timeshare in Spain. He was like the Swedish Chef in *The Muppets*, a super, excited kid. He said, "Hire me and if I'm no good, you can fire me."

Seven years on, his sales skills and leadership get better every year. I attended his wedding in Thailand and recently he moved to help grow our Singapore business. He is now married with a daughter. When he arrived, he had nothing. He still doesn't spend much money on material things and he is the most positively infectious human you could ever meet. He built one of our biggest magazines and fired himself from the role by building up his successor. He accumulated property and shares and is financially very stable. I was so pleased to see him in his beautiful home, sitting contentedly on his veranda overlooking the bay.

After the birth of his daughter, he wanted to spend

more time at home, so he did. He managed time better than anyone I have ever met and his productivity went through the roof. He is a constant reader and always brings fresh ideas to the business. In many ways, he is what Ink stands for: a place to learn, grow, and find ways to do the right thing by others. I built Ink to give others the working environment I craved as a youngster. A place where you run your own business, without the risks and with plenty of rewards.

If you do not take advantage of the opportunities available to you, you will miss out. That's how life works, you need to be ready to perform and sometimes you don't have the luxury to warm up first.

Most of us only realise too late that the sliding doors were open for that nano-second. There are a few things I regret, like not keeping all the property I owned. My gambling brain makes me take profits and had I been a hoarder like some of my friends both in the stock market and real estate, I would be a lot wealthier today. I regret letting a few members of staff slip through the net as we weren't quite ready to help them, and I definitely regret any day that I don't achieve one decent thing.

It's important to remember that every failure is a lesson; you don't learn when things are going well. You learn in reverse: that one thing that might bug you today will be the thing that makes you better further down the line.

To be successful in sales, you need your instincts to be alive. Most over-educated people have had these bashed out of them. That why some of our best are the ones who skipped school or were dropouts from university.

I was manipulated by some people early in business and that experience helped me as I developed. The art of negotiating is not caring if you win or lose. It's hard to negotiate with someone who doesn't care. I am good at getting what I want – call it inane belief, or just sheer chutzpah. I will never waive my right to get a result and I will always do my best to give everyone an upside. I couldn't tell you how many times I was told we don't do that, we don't work that way, that's not how it works around here. It's all nonsense. With your mind set on the goal, everything you want and desire is available to you. Focus on solutions, never the problem.

I have created a really interesting life. It's a life filled with really quirky people, with friends in the weirdest of places, and a Rolodex of people with great influence. I have met and read just about everyone who has had a hand in motivation in the last three decades and I can tell you, if some of the words sound familiar, it's my interpretation of what I learned from all of them. To each and every one of them, thank you for giving me the energy to be the best version of me every day of the week.

Take F'in Action

Create a morning routine that works for you and stick to it! It doesn't need to be yoga at 4am but figure out what ensures a positive and productive start to your day. Understand that your employees' lives will change over the years. Think of ways to support them in this and you can expect loyalty in return.

4

STAY RELEVANT

THIS BOOK AND LIFE are all about the 78% rule. If you understand this statistic you understand how I have stayed in business for so long. You see, this is the number that most businesses don't understand. If tomorrow, 78% of businesses disappeared, no one would really give a fuck. That's the sad fact and every business needs to stay relevant to their followers. As Facebook and Apple found out, even the biggest companies will struggle unless they keep innovating. Our data and digital footprint are becoming more important to us now we realise that companies are using it for whatever the hell they want.

We use this 78% statistic in sales. Simply put, if a business doesn't invest in building or strengthening their brand, someone will come along and offer it cheaper, quicker, or cooler. Brands come and go, and it's the owner's job to keep their brand relevant and alive. Every year many businesses fail. They go backwards and blame market conditions and other crappy reasons. The reality is, no one really needs their product anymore and they had a poor strategy.

As salespeople, it's our job to help brands thrive and find new customers. They have a real problem staying alive in this digital world. No longer do we need to sell what we have, it's our job to help provide solutions to businesses around the globe to stay in business. We need to empower the current generation of business owners to change the way they think about how they promote their companies. We need to help them create strategies that ensure they get the results they want from advertising in whatever medium they choose.

We identify problems and provide solutions – that's what we do. If the customer does not want to listen to our advice, that doesn't make them wrong. If we provide good enough solutions to their problems, they work with us, if we don't, they don't buy – it's as simple as that. Let's not waste time telling people what our product is all about, let's focus on what the product does for them. That's what's important, and if they believe us we have a relationship. Then the real works starts and you have to keep them as a client. We have to under promise and way over deliver.

Take F'in Action

Keep yourself up-to-date with innovation, technology, and the media. Set aside time regularly to read and learn about what is changing in the world. Create a company-wide philosophy so that every employee understands how your customers should be treated. Ensure that from top to bottom, every system and product or service goes through a chain of quality control.

5

SUCCESS IS DRIVEN BY BELIEF

THE ABOVE HAS been my motto since I started. It was also the name of the first book I co-authored about the first ten years of the business. The thing is this: if you do not believe in your product with all your being and heart, the success will only be temporary.

If you are selling what you are selling just for the money, you are doing your clients and your company a major disservice. You have to have the unshakable belief that the product you sell is genuinely good for whoever consumes or purchases it. You have to have more belief in your medium than any of your competitors. So many of my competitors sell at half the prices I do. They just don't believe like I do how good a product it is. They have commoditised it and devalued it.

Don't worry about your lack of experience – believe me, you will get it! I can tell you that, in the process, through every failure and every success, you will build your own core principles and beliefs that will serve you well. It starts with that first step.

Make up your own mind, other opinions don't count. This is your life so live by what you think and believe. The more people you ask for an opinion the more you are relinquishing your right in the decision-making process. You know the right thing to do, you don't need others to give you justification, this is where procrastination and mistakes kick in.

Clients sometimes tell us they don't get a response from a campaign. The issue with this is we never agreed what would or would not be a good outcome before we started. They might want the phone to ring, so they need to make sure the creative tells people to do that. Advertisers use the same creative across multiple touch points, they should target each audience differently, but they don't.

I remember when we launched a magazine for an American airline and a hotel group bought an advert. I happened to be in the office when the rep told our salesperson that the campaign was a disaster and never to darken their door again. Her solution was to give the client a cheap advert to have another go. I said, "Let's look at the process."

I got to work, I looked at the ad – the creative was great, the offer was good. The issue was that when I went through the process, I discovered that the phone number did not work and you could not book the offer. I then called up the customer service and tried to book and they told me that it was not possible. Since then, I investigate every failure as much as I can. There is always a good reason why campaigns don't work.

Another major advertiser called and told me he was going to pull the campaign unless I reduced the price. I said, "Pull it." Two weeks later he phoned in a panic. It turns out we had been generating lots of leads for him and his team had been forwarding them on to their partners. These partners were not following up. He said, "Let's give it one more quarter and I'll respond to the clients myself." Hey presto – he built a huge business, he increased his spend, his model changed and he has been hugely successful. In most media businesses they drop the price to keep the client happy and decide that the product didn't work. In my experience, the product always works – you just don't always get the outcome you wanted. But if you work out what you want going in, you can plan for the desired outcome.

The same can be said for decision-making. Too many people think decisions are only good when you get a good outcome. It's just not true. Many times, I have made great decisions only to get a terrible result.

Please do not base your results on your decisions, as I have had great results off of shitty decisions. Life is simple, make enough good decisions and start with the end in mind and things will fall into place.

When I was twenty-one, I had ripped out an advert and posted it in my kitchen. It was an advert for Sunseeker, the luxury speedboat company. The headline read "Many dream but few achieve." Some twenty years later I hired a Sunseeker from their HQ in Poole for an event. That's a slow return on their investment but that advert did more for me than Sunseeker ever assumed or measured against: it drove me every day that I looked at it. Today, I look at the certificate I got from climbing Kilimanjaro and that reminds me how determined I was that week.

You cannot measure how a campaign works based on short-term results. When clients ask to do a trial, I always ask the same question: "Are you in business for the long or short term?" They will predictably say "long", so I tell them "Stop trading like a short-term business." It's the epidemic of the digital, instant gratification, media world of today. So much money is being wasted chasing things that are just not attainable. A good campaign is a multimedia mix of old and new media, short- and long-term marketing.

The challenge remains that most companies

judge the success of a campaign on the next quarter's results. When someone advertises with us today, they get a mix of long-term inspiration and support of other offline campaigns; they benefit from the fact that passengers enjoy higher recall in the air; they get association of some of the biggest travel brands in the world; and they gain credibility from being among many cool brands that have built their companies using our products. Their staff see their adverts and the bosses are proud as they lean back in their seats.

As I was working on this chapter, a new client called me to say he had only got twenty-two new orders from the campaign. I said, "And?"

"It's not great," he said. My reply was for him to wait and see what happened next. His next call to me was very different. "I didn't get any more orders, but mad things are happening, suppliers saw my ad and my profile has gone up with them and a large retail chain who I have been banging down the door for a year finally will see me. The best bit was a warehouseman stopped me and said he was flying back from his holiday and saw the advert and was so proud to see us in the airline magazine."

That's what we deliver every day – inspiration. You need ridiculous belief that your product will do good for customers and sometimes it's hard to prove

ROI, which I think is the wrong metric to judge marketing on.

We have products in every seat, and on most days six people will sit in each seat. That's hundreds of people on hundreds of planes. Just think about how many planes are in the sky right now, and people are still dipping into the seat-back pocket during the flight. That's real engagement. That's why I believe.

The belief comes from knowledge and experience, from hearing the stories and uncovering the information. It comes from learning from failures, it comes from knowing what you do inside and out. It comes from losing, winning, and taking part.

We aspire to make all our clients a 22% business: one that is relevant, cool, that people love to work for – and with – and to grow, year after year. It's not easy to do.

Take F'in Action

Your customers are your best source of information when it comes to staying ahead of the competition. Check in with them, ask how and where you can improve. Communication is key. Don't let your successes and failures rule your mood. Celebrate the success and praise your team but also take the failures as an opportunity to grow.

6

IT'S OK NOT TO BE OK

SOMETIMES IN LIFE, you won't always feel OK, so I live by the phrase, that it's OK not to be OK. Life doesn't always live up to the high bar we decide to live by. Sometimes life is shit and people don't do the right things to you or for you. People tragically die before they should. And often life just seems to make no sense.

I struggled with many things over the years and being a chest-beating alpha male, I didn't share particularly well. I probably was borderline depressive at times. And this wasn't because I was struggling financially or didn't have love in my life. It's really important to have people who can get you out of your poor state.

To the outside world, I had everything, yet I was unfulfilled and down. I would gamble, I would eat too much, and go to some very dark places mentally. It takes a lot to get back on track when you have been on a bender for a week.

Today, with the support network around me, I do not suffer as much. My coping mechanisms are stronger and I find other ways to return myself to where I need to be. It's not that you can't be sad, just don't spend much time in that place. It's OK not to be OK.

My son asked me recently whether I get sad. And I told him honestly, of course I get sad, I just shift my focus to what will make me feel happy. If it's a problem that's making me feel sad then I focus on finding a solution. Sometimes, people feel sad for a variety of different reasons. Sometimes, they don't really know the reason, just that they feel flat and unhappy and that's okay too. I have times like this too – I just focus on doing the things that I know will take me out of that state of mind. I go for a walk, have a meal with someone I want to spend time with, book a holiday or a treat. I find something and someone that I know will shift my focus. I don't allow myself to stay down for too long.

Knowing that it's OK not to be OK has helped me deal with many things and situations. Nothing runs exactly the way you plan things. Life has a funny way of turning out and as long as you understand that, then challenges, problems, and failures are only events. They are never permanent and they make you who you become. You learn more from things going wrong than you could ever learn if things only went the way you imagined them to. It's also true, the things you dislike doing at work, are actually the things that get you the results you want.

How you see yourself affects how you treat other people. If we feel OK, then our relationships with others thrive. Once upon a time, I would cross the road rather than chat with someone. Today, I am comfortable in my own skin, I can mix and mingle with anyone from any background or experience. In business, I have gone through every phase, so I can talk about what makes businesses tick and what failure looks and feels like. I no longer feel intimidated by anyone or anything and this all stems from this simple phrase and the emotion it brings and confidence it allows me.

If you want to be successful, make sure you understand business; understand the challenges businesspeople face; learn how to read a set of accounts, be a solution-driven human and stop worrying about anything and everything. Worrying doesn't make things better, it just creates a negative future. Be an optimist, they believe the future is bright and exciting even if they have no idea how to make it happen. And finally work bloody hard. Nothing beats hard work. No one is going to give you something for nothing and they won't keep giving you anything unless you keep delivering. Remember this: you are only as good as your next deal.

It's your time to own your own happiness, so enjoy your journey. It's only yours and no one can enjoy it for you. Celebrate every win no matter how small and remember this: in every interaction with people it's what you leave in them, not what you leave with them. People will always remember what you did for them, both good and bad.

Take F'in Action

Remember, a bad work day is just a bad day. Tomorrow could be your best day ever. Don't take your home stress to work and vice-versa. Your employees and your family don't deserve to deal with your external issues so create a mindset change routine. Maybe you hit the gym between work and home or meet with a supportive friend for coffee at lunch.

7

IT'S ALL ABOUT TIME

SPEND TIME WITH PEOPLE who believe what you believe, life is about who you keep in your company. They say – whoever they are – that you are a reflection of the five people you spend the most time with. Don't be the cleverest person in the room. If you are, you are definitely in the wrong room. Over the years, I have cut myself off from people who did not add value to my life.

In life, you need a few close friends, a loving family, and some great acquaintances. That's it. Life is not Facebook – just because you were in school together or were once very close doesn't mean you have to be friends for life.

Early in my journey, I figured out million-second thinking. A million seconds is approximately eleven days and if you use time sensibly you can achieve everything you would in a month within eleven days. That way, you could double your productivity every single month.

Time is the only commodity we are not getting

any more of. Once it's gone, it's gone. Working with so many millennials, they really do not value time and waste so much. Too much time spent on screens, worrying why no one has liked the picture they posted ten minutes ago. As you get older you start to appreciate time so much more, you stop wasting it and start being mean with people who do.

Everyone talks about time management and how to be good at it. It's nonsense. How do you manage time? You can't create any more of it. I don't think it's about time management, it's about managing the tasks in a better way. Focusing only on the things that are really important and not being busy fools. We spent many years busy, being really busy. Once we focused on the most important products, on products that made money, we found ourselves more time which we used more effectively and we started making more money.

You also need to find time for you. Yes, you. Without you investing in you, there will not be a you to do all these things for others. It's very easy to do so much for other people but if you are not looking after the most important person you will burn out, you will get depressed, and you will be useless to everyone around you.

Being in a business that is private-equity backed,

they always want growth and the growth drive never ends. I guess that's why we have survived for so long. We have grown and grown and the only way to keep doing that is to use time effectively: being agile, nimble, and surrounding yourself with the best team you can build.

Take F'in Action

Monitor what you do with your time for eleven days. You might be surprised to find you are wasting hours every week on social media when you could be far more productive in your business and you may even carve out enough time to learn a new skill. Make a commitment to yourself to network with people who are smarter, more successful, and happier than yourself going forward. Find time for you.

8

BUILDING A GREAT TEAM

HIRE PEOPLE WHO believe what you believe. If you want to achieve much in life, the simplest way is to help enough people to achieve what they want. If you want wealth, help others get wealthy, if you want accolades, get your team winning awards. Whatever it is you want, get it for somebody else in the process.

Recruitment had always been a challenge for my business. Early in 2006, I sat at the Kellogg School of Management in Chicago in an executive education course. The professor, Andy Zoltners, asked the class what attrition was like in our businesses and most of the answers were single digit responses. He came to me and when I said 87%, he spat his coffee across the classroom. He asked how I felt about that? I said, "It's not high enough yet." The room filled with laughter and I was gifted a Kellogg polo shirt at the end of the course. I am sure he still uses my story today.

I explained that I felt he had asked the wrong question. I said, "Ask me how many of my good people left?" Which was, in fact, zero. He surmised that we had interviewing issues. I listened and spent a lot of time and effort improving all my teams' skills at interviewing. We had training, we did more profiling, we even learned to read handwriting – which I think is one of the best skills I have ever accumulated. No longer could anyone just fib their way through an interview with me.

Today, we have much lower attrition, people enjoy what we do and we do some crazy stuff. Incentives to the best places on the planet, private jet trips, Michelin-starred restaurants, and shopping trips across the globe. Every time I go somewhere that I love, I make sure I arrange a staff incentive for that place. I want everyone to enjoy the destinations that I enjoy. The more we give back to the team, the harder they work for our clients.

I've built a great team over the years. They have worked and played as hard as anyone I could have wished for, and we have created a trust and a bond that has improved over that time. I am gruff and have high expectation leadership, but we reward staff well and I make sure we all spend time reflecting, re-creating, and thinking outside of the office.

Over the last four years, our trips have taken us to Dubai, Cape Town, Columbia, Utah, and Vegas.

With hindsight, if you play hard, people do work much harder for you. What we spend on training and coaching today is what we used to spend in a decade. It's helping us grow and support each other.

In the last couple of years, we have invested so much in coaching, both individual and group. We have full-time performance coaches in all our offices, sports psychologists who come in a couple of times a week, a masseur, yoga classes, and many other additional services to make sure people's well-being is supported. Mental health is such an important issue today and even 300lb men still get down in the dumps and need pulling out. It's very easy to focus on what you don't have, instead of celebrating what you do.

Ninety percent of my senior management team has been through our GOO programme (Grow Our Own) and we have got better at hiring senior staff and helping them grow into our unique culture. Over the years, people have ridiculed us for the way we do energy sessions in the morning and afternoon and they have criticized us for micromanagement. Now, people are doing case studies on how we do things and how our sales infrastructure works.

There's a well-known quote from an American trade unionist that sums it up: "First they ignore you, then they laugh at you, then they fight you, then you win." Today, we are winning so much business and I attribute this to time and perseverance. The longer you stay in business, the more successful you become.

We used to have a young guy in our US office who was such a hard worker, he would pitch hard every day. His pitch was good and his storytelling was great, but after about nine months he threw in the towel. The following year, the phone would ring with people who were then ready to buy. Salespeople give up too soon – selling is a long game and those that can stick at it get the results, normally from people who have done the hard work for them. I always say it doesn't matter if people leave, the relationships and spend has always been with the airlines, not just them. People do buy from people but more importantly, they buy great products.

We hired some really experienced people and they spent a lot of time, money, and entertaining budget trying to get business across the line and they failed. They were focused too much on relationships and not enough on actually telling stories and helping clients fix problems. This is the reason people buy anything, it's to fix a problem.

My tip for anyone would be hire slowly and fire quickly. When you get it wrong, deal with it quickly.

If people are doing the right things, work with them. I take failures personally. When people leave, I always want to understand where we went wrong. Sometimes they don't want to do the job they signed up for, sometimes they are just not good enough, and sometimes we let them down.

Take F'in Action

Take each area of your business and break it down. What can be improved upon, how can you support the people in that department to do their job better, what preparations may need to be put in place for future changes? Society and people and laws are always changing and businesses need to change with them. Have a regular check-in policy where you look at every aspect of your business and life. Circle a date in your calendar each year and make time for this.

9

WHO WILL INSPIRE YOU?

THIS IS ONE of the questions I ask of all salespeople. After all, I can only go so far in making them better. Personal investment, reading, watching videos, going to conferences, events, and reading more is so important if you want to get better. Reach out and talk to the people who inspire you. I have met and chatted with so many people who have inspired me over the years. They normally will welcome hearing from you and helping you.

I once called out motivational speaker Simon Sinek at a conference he was speaking at in London and this led to a one-on-one with him and he came and visited us in London. Even the busiest and most successful people on the planet will help you if you only have the courage to ask. If you are inspired by my story, Google me, write to me, and I will always give you the best advice I can.

As I am writing this chapter, I have two LinkedIn messages thanking me for help I gave recently.

Sometimes, you never know the impact you will have on others – both positive and negative – but whichever one, hopefully, will drive them to do more and get better.

I feel like I have the perfect job, it's probably the job I would do even if I wasn't getting paid to do it. I love working with people – especially young people – and I love helping them get better and fulfilling their dreams.

Every year at Christmas, I make my team write a letter to themselves, dated the following New Year's Eve. It's written from the future and describes what they've achieved the following year. We have been doing this for ten years and I have to tell you that the people who have been doing this for a while are creating the most incredible years.

The action of putting it down on paper starts a signal in the brain and soon the behaviours change and you make things happen. I used this for the private jet trip for my birthday. Once it was in there, the mind got to work and finds a way to make that achievement happen.

Every year, so many people achieve so much more, just through inspiring themselves by putting it down on paper. Normally, we need to push back and get many rewritten so they are specific with exactly what they want. The scarier the better and the bigger the ask, the bigger the response. Last year, someone put down they would do a £1m deal and in December £1.4 arrived – it was incredible!

My favourite one was a lady who wanted to move to New York and she put a date in her letter saying that would be the date she would move. She did move to New York, which I was delighted about. She rang me a few months later as she was tidying her papers and said the date she had put in her letter a year earlier had been the exact date she boarded the plane!

Salespeople need to be kinder to themselves, they really do put themselves under more pressure than any employer will ever do. They set themselves unfair expectations. These are unrealistic goals and they then get down when they miss them. It's our job to ensure they have the skills and coaching so that they can deliver what they expect.

I also think businesses put unfair expectations on themselves to give employees the best experience. We attempt to give them the best job, great tools, fun, incentives and most of the time it's never enough.

A lot of the time, the pressure cooker and high targets they set themselves are the reason they fail – not because the company didn't deliver. Every sales job has targets and high expectations, if they don't, don't expect the business to be around for too long.

I always say to my team, "Be kind to yourself." No matter how good you are, you are never as good as you can be. It doesn't matter how good you are, it's how good you can be that matters. We all have much to learn. I really don't think I know very much and every day I find ways to learn something new. If I am not growing, I'm stagnating and that, for me, is just another word for dying.

One of the other things I realised was HR (human resources) needed to be realigned. In its place, we needed RH (resourcing humans). It was imperative to give them the skills and resources to do their job. The whole HR function was out-of-date and the once-a-year appraisal was just a cry for a pay rise. As a business, I was working closely with the teams and this funnelled down the line, so everybody knew what people needed on a daily and weekly basis. We got closer to their needs and were more in tune with their moods.

Giving your teams the ability to make decisions is fine but you need to allow them to make mistakes and learn. You cannot blame people for making decisions if you are not cool with them making mistakes. Give your team all the necessary weapons to go to battle.

Despite this thinking, I know I am not perfect and it continues to take a lot of tweaking and adjusting to get things better. Invest in yourself, increase your value, and you will always be in demand.

The interview process is the best example of selling. The candidate comes in and tells you all about the product (them) and then proceeds to spout features and benefits ("I am really motivated and I love people, clients love me, and I'm really hardworking.") without offering any solution to fix the problem the business has.

The perfect interview goes a bit like this – candidate walks in and says, "Hey there, you need someone who will be wonderful to manage, someone who will always be positive and inspire all those around them, and be a great ambassador for the business. I will be the first in and last out and be a pleasure to be around. Your clients, they will love me and recommend me to their friends. Whatever target you set me, I will smash it and if you put it up, I will rise to the challenge." Me – "When can you start?"

I have interviewed over one thousand people and to this day, never has anyone given me a solution to my problem.

Take F'in Action

Ask for help or mentoring from people in a position you'd like to see yourself in a year, five years, ten years, and so on. Likewise, offer help to those following you. Write down and verbalise your goals. Put dates against them to keep yourself working towards them. Encourage your team to do the same.

10

THE SALES PROCESS

WHEN I WAS TURNING OVER $2m, I kept getting told my system would not work as we got bigger, the same at $20m, and now as we reach $100m I'm still being told it's not the way to do it. Don't do what everyone else is doing, don't follow the herd because you think that's the right way to do business. Selling is very simple, it's us that overcomplicate it.

My favourite story was a $2m deal with one of the largest car companies in the world. There was no presentation, no doughnuts, no agency visit – just a great story, a picture, and a supportive person at the client side. When the campaign was in full force, the European marketing manager said to me, "How did you make this happen? This would have needed twenty people to sign this off and should have taken weeks if not months. You did this over a weekend."

Let's start at the beginning, talk to people who can make things happen in any business. Even before that, it's all about lead sourcing. It doesn't matter what you sell, you need good-quality leads. I guess watching the film about real estate salesmen, *Glengarry Glen Ross*, was when I began my sales career, I had the leads drummed into me. I spend so much time training my team to be the best lead sourcers on the planet, although we call it treasure hunting, as some people hate the idea of lead sourcing. I say, you need to love lead sourcing as much as you love breathing.

One of my many chairmen told me once it was the special sauce in the business. As a publishing veteran, he had never seen anyone push lead sourcing as I did. Wherever I am, from watching a soccer match, to walking down any street, all I ever do is look for companies. There are millions of businesses on the planet desperate to grow, to stay relevant. If we don't find them and help them grow, we are not doing our job right. I still battle with my investors about what makes a good company.

Don't do what everyone else would do. When one of our products was not selling, a few of us brainstormed and decided to put up the price by ten times. What happened was sales increased, revenues boomed and years later this product is still one of our most profitable divisions. All because we were illogical.

Once upon a time, you were judged by the number

of big brands that you worked with. Today's media landscape has changed so much and most of the time it's companies outside the top ten who have the urge and the spend to get bigger. Every day, we see tens of thousands of brands looking for our attention; our job is to help these businesses stand out from the noise. We need to help them increase sales, so they have more to ply back into marketing. There are so many companies slashing budgets, and that just tells me what they are doing is not working. Many of our bigger advertisers are buying more than ever from us because we are clearly helping them achieve those sales targets.

So, once you have the leads, how good is your story? Don't pick up the phone or visit them and waffle on about how good you and your brand are, yada, yada, yada. You need to find their pain points, you need to find out what itch they need scratching. No longer is it relevant to sell what we have, it's our job to figure out what we have that can help them achieve what they want to achieve.

There are so many acronyms for the sales process, they bore me senseless. If you do not understand the challenges a business faces, you cannot help them. A hotel is not going to buy new linen if the rooms and yield they are getting for those rooms are not high enough. However, if they promote they now have special linen, could this help them fill the rooms? Be a creative thinker, give people the solution because there are already enough people focusing on problems. Find out what they need, make sure you understand it, check it back with them, and then give them your recommendations. Be an expert and give great advice.

People buy from people they like and trust? Not true. People buy if they think you will solve a problem for them. I have bought lots of things from people I disliked enormously. Conversely, my print salesman was one of the nicest men I have ever met – he took me racing, he bought me cigars and fancy lunches, but when he couldn't match the price of his competitors, our relationship sadly ended. He regrets it to this day and we remain friends. Don't fool yourself. There are many reasons people buy and don't buy, and most sales calls end up with a NO. If you get disappointed by this, you should not be in sales.

It's so much better to get a NO than a maybe. Maybe is the worst outcome. People are too polite to say no, so they keep you with a false sense that the deal might still happen. Push for NO. Don't get down when you don't sell and don't get too excited when you do.

Just keep improving your knowledge and enhancing your skills, read plenty and learn everything there is to know about the industry you are selling in. Read the journals, go to every event, read the trade press, and speak to every company from A-Z, and no matter how many times you hear NO, keep going back.

The average CMO only lasts about eight months, things change, situations change. Realise the story you used wasn't strong enough and come up with a better story. Find information on their market and share it with them, for no other reason than being useful. Send them handwritten cards, send updates on what you are doing; just never, ever stop keeping in touch with them unless they tell you never to darken their door ever again. And even then, keep an eye out for when they move jobs... and start again with their replacement.

A couple of questions I love that we use during this process, which help me find out how good a job you have done are:

Can you tell me what you love about this idea?

When we go ahead, what would you promote and what would the campaign focus on?

Use NLP. If you don't know what NLP is, Google it and learn it, and really study the chapter in this book on language. There is no big section on closing, if you do the right things in the process, just ask for the business. They will tell you what they want to do. I hate hard closers, you don't need it, you just need to fix the problem. There are loads of closing techniques and I could write pages on them, but you only need them when you don't do the sales process properly and that's not the way to sell. If they say NO, it just means the story wasn't good enough. Go back to stage one and follow through again. Price is very rarely the reason people don't buy.

There is also no such thing as rejection. People might not want what you have to offer right now but there are always plenty of people who will. You just have not found the problem to fix. One of my colleagues always reminds me of his first day selling, when he pitched a company and the guy told him he had no budget. The next day, his colleague next to him pitched the same guy, the same product and before my colleague could say, "Don't bother they have already blown me out," he closed the deal. He was far more persistent after that.

Selling is simple, I was taught KISS – Keep It Simple Stupid. I still use this to run our business. Keep everything simple – simple processes, simple systems and very little will go wrong.

Understand the difference between objection and rejection – only good salespeople get this. Are they objecting to you or rejecting you?

Most objections are buying signals and most rejections are because you have not done your homework properly. One young lady told me she hated rejection. When I pointed out that she wasn't getting rejected, but facing some objections her mindset changed. The main reason people say NO, is because we have not fixed their problem. Simple.

Take F'In Action

Treat each potential customer as an individual, find their pain point, and show them how you can solve it. Don't overcomplicate things for your customers. Go through your processes and check everything works and that it's simple. And if you still get NO, repeat again.

11

YOU'LL NEVER WIN ANYTHING WITH KIDS

OVER THE YEARS, I have been criticised for hiring the inexperienced and young. It's driven by my desire to make a real difference, to help people achieve what they did not think was possible in their lives. For them to give back to those that either sacrificed for them or let them down in some way. I was accused of hiring people no one else might hire, the ones who were slightly damaged or had suffered injustice. I just wanted to find people who wanted to achieve something, people who need someone to believe in them and make them great.

I looked for people who had a real point to prove to someone, who were genuinely hungry to make something of their lives. We hired people that others would ignore and dismiss. We were and remain slightly out of the norm, whatever the norm is. We were, and are, as Steve Jobs said, "The crazy ones, the misfits, the rebels, the troublemakers." I certainly was a very rotund peg in a square hole!

There was a famous footballing pundit who said of the Manchester United team that, "You'll never win anything with kids." And boy, did he eat humble pie as they went on to win trebles and trophy after trophy. My critics, who in part have been directors, shareholders, and employees, all knew a better way than the way I believed in, but the results have proven I was doing something right. Everyone always knows how to run the business better than you. What they need to understand is that it's not like running a bath when you run a company. The key assets are human ones and people are fickle and emotional and have lots of challenges in their lives that you have no control over. You can't just turn a tap on and expect the same temperature time after time.

It takes time to develop people and people are impatient and want instant gratification. Investors and shareholders are impatient and think if you hire more experienced people, you get quicker results. You don't get the longevity we have enjoyed with impatience. The process I have instilled in this business is all about the long game, the learning process and the challenge of never-ending improvement.

I always reflect on the way we do things and I do believe even if I had the opportunity to do it all again, I would not change much. I would still invest heavily in people, I would just find even more people who believe what I believe.

Take F'In Action

Remember, for every piece of advice given, someone else is out there disproving it. You can train someone well who is hungry and believes what you believe. Create opportunities and be patient.

12

LANGUAGE AND POSITIVE THINKING ARE SO IMPORTANT

TO ME, THIS PROBABLY is the most important chapter in the book. So bookmark it and keep coming back to it.

In our business we don't use the words 'hope', 'trying', 'can't', 'but' etc. We remove limiting language and focus on what we *can* do. Having studied NLP (you should have Googled it by now), it's clear we can use words so powerfully. Your brain has no idea if you are lying or telling the truth. "I'm tired, I'm done, I can't do any more." Whatever you tell it, your brain will believe.

No matter how tired or even exhausted you are, you still have 50-60% more to give. I love this stat, and it's probably made up, most stats are. But I use this and very quickly you can go from feeling tired to having so much more energy. I'll talk later about all the gruelling things I have put myself through to prove this and prove to anyone that I have ever worked with what the human body is capable of. It all stems from the mind, the language we use, the voices in our head that, if we control, can make us superhuman individuals.

Another stat I quote is that if you improve your language and grammar, your IQ improves dramatically. (I don't remember the percentage but the important thing is that it improves!) It's so important that you listen to your calls, listen back to what you are saying, and keep adjusting and improving it. Like anyone who is in a performance position, you have to review and look at multiple ways of getting better. Start using your words to create the world you want to live in. In every interaction, the one who has the strongest belief and better use of words wins. Don't be afraid to question everything.

Ask yourself, "Is that really true?" Use assumptive language and point people in the direction you want them to go. Speak with authority, like you own the place and people will soon take notice. Never use hysterical language, for example, "It's a disaster, the documents weren't signed by 6 pm." Is it a disaster? Be very careful with the language you use. Change the words, remove 'fear', 'worry', and 'stress' and replace with 'excited' – it changes the whole meaning.

I always ask people who complain about stress if they go to the gym? They invariably say yes and most enjoy it. I say, "You understand what you are doing at the gym – you are stressing your body, you are tearing your muscles, so they break down and rebuild. That's OK, is it? It's all in the interpretation – you don't mind stressing yourself for a great body, so why do you mind stressing yourself for a great career and life?" Pressure is a privilege and as long as you frame what you say and feel in the right way, your whole situation will change very quickly. There is nothing wrong with being in a bad mood, just don't stay there too long.

Believe in yourself – would you be surprised if I told you that you are the most amazing human being on the planet? Well, you are. Record yourself a message and play it to yourself every day.

"Hi me, you know what, you are such an incredible person, so well respected, such an expert in your field, your customers adore you, your friends cherish every word you say and they love spending time with you. If I could spend a couple of hours with you every day, they would be the best days of my life."

You can adjust to your particular taste but you get the idea. If someone left this message on your answer phone, your shoulders would go back and your chest would puff out and you would be better at whatever it is you do. That's the power of words and language.

Every morning, I would go into my local coffee

shop and the barista would say, "The usual?" And I would reply, "I don't want anything usual, I want exceptional." It's simple examples of shifting language that can shift your thinking, your day, and your mood.

I always tell anyone who will listen, never ever let a snapshot in time be a portrait of your life. You are capable of being incredible, just use the right words, send the right messages to your brain and you will never be disappointed by the results. One bad thing in the morning doesn't make a bad day; one bad moment is exactly that, move forward.

Stories are so important, don't tell yourself shit stories, these are the nonsense you spout when things don't go the way you want them to. They are not true, they are just your brain lying to you again. Make sure your stories are a Hollywood blockbuster where you are the star, never a chorus or a bit-part player. Make sure it has a happy ending and you get the boy or girl of your dreams. Don't create a drama, they never turn out so well. And as you see the credits roll, imagine yourself at the top. It's thinking positively that creates positive moments in life. And as life is made up of many moments, create as many positive ones as you can.

It's really important to understand that sometimes you can't do something. If you add 'yet' to the end of that sentence, it wires the brain to remind you that, with a little practice, you can do anything you want. The same goes for material things – I don't have that car, watch, or whatever... yet!

Take F'in Action

You may have annual training, monthly targets, and appraisals for your employees but what do you have in place for yourself? Find ways of monitoring your own productivity and success – invest in developing yourself. Change your mindset from 'I can't do this' to 'How can I get this done?' Ask yourself better questions.

13

MOTIVATION AND INCENTIVES

HOW MUCH DOES it really work sending our salespeople on amazing trips away or bringing in a masseur once a week? The truth is, there is no way of proving the effectiveness. Even improvement in numbers doesn't mean much, as that might have happened anyway. The truth is this, the more you do to make your environment more interesting, the more people will be engaged. They share on social media, it makes them proud, it makes them feel like they are being treated differently to their friends who don't get any of these perks.

I compare it to cleaning your teeth: you do it every day but you never know at which point it actually works. It's the habit of doing things repeatedly, that's the reason things work, be it exercise, diet, or love. Small habits, done for long periods of time, deliver long-lasting results. And even then, you can always improve it with better toothpaste.

I have been lucky in that over the past twenty-plus

years, my partners have allowed me to experiment with many things to make my sales floor better. Some have delivered and some were a flop. The first masseur I brought in was inappropriate with some of the girls: great masseur, shocking service! We did a weekly "Don't forget your toothbrush," where everyone on the floor would bring their passport and suitcase on Friday morning and one of them would get on a flight to New York with their partner that night.

In the year of writing this book, I sent a girl to Hong Kong in her first month. She left shortly afterwards – these perks doesn't always make them stay. I believe in paying it forward and there are lots of people who have been with me a long time and love the opportunity the incentives have given them to see parts of the world they would never have seen. Don't get me wrong, I have been left disappointed by people's lack of gratitude as well, not even a thank you – they believe it was what they deserved. All I will tell you is there is nothing stranger than people. And gratitude is always appreciated, whatever it might be for.

The getaways at senior levels definitely helped us bond together, we achieved so much more as a team and I have watched these guys mature and improve so much. They have developed since we started these initiatives. The last one we did, we went to the Lake District, stayed in youth hostels and did yoga in the rain – I'm pretty sure they will prefer their next trip to Sri Lanka.

The funniest incentive we ever did was watching five German girls attempting to spend $1,000 each at an outlet mall in New York. They were either amazing at it or spent three days going back and forth because they couldn't make their minds up. Either way, it was an experience I will never forget, feeling the excitement of them running riot through Ralph Lauren, Burberry, and Prada.

One of the greatest things we used to do each year was to take part in the David Beckham inter-company tournament. It was a fundraiser every Christmas. Some of the guys told me this was the greatest day of the year and even their life. It was a chance to play with a footballing legend and be managed by a current player. Each team got to have a picture and have Becks sign their shirt, and with sixteen teams it meant there was footballing heaven for one night. We never won it but while it existed, it was a great night for the boys and some of the girls. Becks is in Miami now and is regularly at our offices, as that's where his sponsors are for Inter Miami. Next time, I might propose to him we bring it back in the

USA. (I should have put that in my Christmas letter to myself.)

My fourth son, George, was born on 20th December, 2007. I left the hospital soon after he was born just so I could play in the tournament, that's how much fun it was. Thankfully, my wife was supportive and relished the alone time with her newborn.

The furthest incentive was to New Zealand and Australia from London and San Diego from Singapore. The US and Singapore teams would regularly visit each other too. The most expensive was the private jet incentive and a Michelin-starred lunch. Stupid things too, like the Ink Wheel of Fortune and the opportunity to win a coffee, $20, or lunch with me were just as effective. I sent people to football and rugby World Cup finals where they saw their national teams play. We did Super Bowl multiple times and we did lots of incentives around the London Olympics where we brought loads of people in to watch events. We played beach volleyball against the GB girls and I will never forget the atmosphere sitting watching them play during the competition. I gave away a car (that had some bad tax benefits for the winner), Vegas dozens of times (always fun when the adult awards are on), Cuba, Cancun, Ibiza, and Miami over five times each.

We sent people to Svalbard, the top of the world, Cape Town at the bottom, and with New Zealand and Argentina, we basically covered the globe. This year we are sending a team paintballing in Pablo Escobar's house in Columbia.

Sometimes, it costs us a pretty penny in tax bills. The business has continued to grow aggressively and I imagine as long as we continue to deliver, the fun and games will continue. I believe they add that special X factor to the culture.

I am a believer that if you work hard, you play harder. Everyone enjoys the pressure when it comes, because the end game is an enjoyable experience.

Take F'in Action

Find ways to create incentives. They don't need to be big, or expensive, or flashy but even a cup of coffee can be appreciated. My top tip is to incentivise for the right reasons, not just for an instant pick up in business. Sometimes, it can take weeks or even months after the incentive to see results and every now and then there are no results – no F'in sales.

14

ALL ABOUT THE HABITS

TO PERFORM WELL you need to instil great habits – my routine now is much better than it has ever been. I spend time with people who are better than me and am always on the lookout for many more. I get through books like a champion (to be fair, mostly of the audio variety) and spend copious amounts of time watching stuff that helps my mind improve. I study stocks and company performances and I want to understand how great CEOs think and behave.

Sleep is more important than most people realise. If you are not getting the right sleep or you don't have the right pillows and mattresses, you are holding yourself back. Spend more than you would even think about spending.

I do fasting, I love colonics, and cryotherapy, I love investigating what can make me perform better. I am fifty years old and over 300lbs, but I train all week, play soccer at the weekend, kickbox, and still have a full head of my own hair. People marvel at my energy, despite my weight. I play tennis at a good standard and play golf terribly, yet I persist.

My biggest challenge is that I love food. No, I adore food. I eat too much, so no matter all the other good stuff I do, I ruin it with food. And despite a good attempt at curbing it, the weight drops off and then returns like a decent boomerang. I just haven't found the right path to drop that 50lbs and keep it off – YET!

It's really important to not just train up to your neck but work your brain as much as you can do, really challenge yourself to learn more. My formal education finished at sixteen but I have never stopped learning and never will. I have no ambition to retire, it's like watching people melt. So many business people who were once dynamic suddenly collapse as soon as they switch their brain off. I love working and I love not working, it's what inspires me daily. You need to listen to your body, like a fancy car, you need to know when to recreate or as I call it re-create. As I said before, work hard but relax harder and find time to really think. Thinking is one of the most undervalued pastimes.

People talk about a work-life balance; what they mean is they want to be stimulated as much at home as they are at work and, because they are not, therefore they don't have the right balance. No, you just don't have the right partner. There cannot ever be balance, you need to allocate your time and energy to things that you want to do the most. Doing yoga doesn't help the relationship at home or work but it centres you. I was always told live your life like the Mercedes logo – you, your friends and family, and work in three equal measures.

How many of you reading this do that? We are all skewed towards work. And, by the way, I don't know anyone that has balance – it's an ideal, just be present with whoever you are around. I know and meet lots of successful people in my life, I have never met anyone who feels balanced.

One other habit I love is juicing – fresh ginger shots and wheatgrass get my day off to a great start. When I am in the States, the money I spend in the juice bars is insane.

I love to gamble, I don't smoke, other than the odd cigar or shisha, and drink rarely. I am happiest sat at my desk or on a beach chair. I am addicted to the phone, and maybe it's time to talk about the damage that technology is doing to us.

Take F'in Action

Join a business book club and make an effort to introduce yourself but listen to what people are telling you. People will often willingly share their 'pain points' and you may be able to solve them and create a new customer. Ask for recommendations from anyone successful in your opinion. They may suggest a development course or even introduce you to someone important. Sit in libraries and bookstores and look for inspiration. People-watching can be surprisingly valuable.

15

THE PHONE AND SOCIAL MEDIA

THE PHONE IS the greatest invention of the 21st century and the worst. At the Pope's inauguration in 2005 the crowd stood in amazement as the Pope was installed. Yet, at Pope Francis' ceremony in 2013, the same image shows everyone on their phones taking pictures and videoing the experience.

I recently went to a world heavyweight boxing match and, as the boxers came out, everyone was filming. Pictures are great mementos, but real memories are even more valuable. Enjoy the moments!

The biggest challenge is with social media, as it presents a picture that everyone has a perfect life but you. Others are doing amazing things while you are feeling sorry for yourself. None of this is true – it's all just sad people, doing their best to make themselves feel good – but it's causing so much harm, creating depression in teenagers and adults. Something needs to happen, depression has overtaken every terrible disease and it's not slowing down.

Once, after a long day's work in Singapore I was walking towards the lift with a colleague. This guy in front of me was walking so slowly while he checked his phone, so I said to him, "Can't you put that down for one second?" He hurriedly put his phone in his pocket and agreed. As we walked out the lift my colleague asked me what this man did in the business, I said that he didn't. I'd never seen him before.

It's a bugbear of mine watching people on the street glued to their phones walking so slowly, or lovers sat at dinner on their phones. We were just as bad on a recent holiday where at times all of us were on our phone around the breakfast table. It's really not helping us and we all need to get off the devices more often every day. I now switch mine off an hour before I go to bed and don't open it until my day begins. I am getting better at not having it in meetings and get grumpy when people are on their phones when they shouldn't be.

Use it to take a picture every day and use it for notes and dictation. In meetings, especially when you are talking to someone, put it away – out of sight. We have to improve real listening, conscious listening, and we cannot do that with a phone anywhere near us. What does it say to the person in front of you when you sit down for a meal or meeting, then bring out your phone and place it on the table. It says, I'm here with you physically but I'm just going to keep that door slightly ajar for a more interesting/important conversation or message.

Texts and email responses on the phone can be dangerous too. If it's negative or upsetting, don't react, it doesn't help the situation and invariably makes it a damn sight worse. I have been caught out reacting too many times.

In the past twelve months, despite enjoying the best year of my life, the most travelled and the most fun, I didn't post one thing on social media. To me, it's showing off and I don't need to show off to anyone but myself. I am not doing anything for anyone but me and my family. I don't need to tell the world what I am doing, what I had for breakfast, that my kids are not well, or my dog is at the vet, and how much I love my wife. I talk to some of my friends who post aggressively and they see this as their way of giving two fingers up to the world. We disagree regularly about this.

I was recently made aware that someone was still tormented by me from our time at school together. I found them on Facebook and apologised. I also realised there were literally hundreds of people waxing lyrical about things that happened over thirty-five years ago. Those who live in the past or the future just don't live anywhere and life is always being compared to another time.

My kids communicate via Snapchat and Instagram and businesses are attempting to run their companies based on response to social media. Even the US president seems to be running the country through Twitter.

The things that the world has created to make us stronger and more efficient are also probably making us weaker and ineffective. I think phones and social media fall into this category. They are creating so much more anxiety than they were designed to do. Fake news is not a new phenomenon but having something in our hand so many hours a day, that is listening and hacking our lives, cannot be a recipe for good.

Life through a lens is sometimes distorted – enjoy the moments and enjoy spending time in real conversation. I have had some amazing conversations over the last couple of years, with many extremely wise people who were very generous with their time. Build trust, be human, and stand out from all the automated noise.

Take F'in Action

If you receive bad news, take time to calm down before you respond. Even if it wasn't your fault at all, consider what you can do in future to make sure it doesn't reach that stage. Next time you are at an event, concert, or one of your children's school performances, be in the present. Enjoy with your eyes as well, not just through a lens.

16

RANDOM ACTS OF KINDNESS, MAGIC MOMENTS

IT'S REALLY EASY to get carried away by how amazing things are going and then forget to do things for others. I won't pass a charity box without putting in my loose change and I will support anyone that asks me to support them, if they are doing it for a good cause.

I have made sure as a business we give as much as we can and for my staff to work with homeless shelters, food kitchens, or anything else we can do to make people's lives a bit easier. We buy hoodies for the homeless in winter, we cross the Sahara every year raising thousands for various charities, we dress up. I remember the time when all the boys wore dresses from charity shops for a day – the picture of four guys peeing in their dresses will be an image hard to remove from my brain and I certainly don't need an iPhone to remember that! Our charity work is really important to me. We have been blessed and it's everyone's duty to help those who have not been as lucky.

On trips to San Francisco, San Diego, Rio, Cape Town, I made sure my team and kids all spent time going to the rough parts of town to see and help where they could. Apart from helping others, I think it's good for your soul to give as much as you can, even sometimes giving more than you can.

Life is a collection of moments and I say to everyone I interact with, "Let's create magical moments, let's do things people can never thank us for. Let's do things out of the kindness of our hearts." Send flowers to your loved ones for no reason. Buy a coffee for the next person in line. This was an interesting experiment: I encouraged my team one day, for everyone to buy someone in line a cup of coffee and funnily enough straight afterwards when they returned to the office good things would start happening, deals would start dropping. It's ironic, yet things like that get people excited to give more – not always for the right reason but at least the right result.

We write handwritten letters, send thank you cards, remember people's birthdays and their Inkerversaries, which is the date they joined the company. We celebrate births, engagements, and I have attended several weddings and sadly funerals too. I believe it's so important to support your clients and your teammates in good and in tough times.

I'm sure all the good things we do will be remembered after we are gone. It's about creating your legacy, doing the right things as often as you can. We are nowhere near perfect and I have upset lots of people over the years, but my intentions are always to make people better.

Take F'in Action

Run an annual charity event in your business, be it a clothing donation drive, adrenalin challenges or mental health awareness. Commit to a thirty-day kindness challenge. Regularly check in with friends and loved ones. Instead of "how are you?" ask "What can I do to make your day better?" or "How can I brighten your day?"

17

CHALLENGING THE CRITICS

DON'T BELIEVE THE fake news. "Worse than hell," said one reviewer of us on the employment review website Glassdoor. Back in 2013, our rating was so terrible that any positive review on the platform was labelled as 'fake', while all the negative ones were deemed 100% accurate.

As a rule, we employ lots of first jobbers at Ink and we especially need self-starters. Over the years, I have learnt that some people require more hand-holding than we could cope with. And over a certain period, our reviews got worse and worse. My HR team used this as a reason for not being able to hire the right people. We contacted Glassdoor about these comments – some were so outrageous, and others were against their own policies, yet they would not take them down.

So, I decided to take the matter into my own hands and posted a completely fabricated review of my time working at Glassdoor. Amazingly, they posted it and it stayed up for about a week until I wrote a blog about it and believe me, they quickly took it down. The problem with Glassdoor is that all the reviews are anonymous, no checks or balances are taken to see if the person ever worked there.

My head of recruitment went about getting all our satisfied employees to comment. We responded to every negative review and really did some listening and did our best to clean up our support systems. We upped the hours of the life coaches and ensured that we had full-time support and training experts on-hand to help onboard people, as well as improving the exit interviews for anyone who chose to leave. And within a short period of time, we were listed as one of the best places to work in media. How wonderful is that?

The negativity reduced and positive reviews continued. So, I guess it's fair to say that every business has the odd ex-employee who lashes out, but the point is to ensure you have done everything you can. Generally, you will find that it's about them and not about you.

Sadly today, people can lie, be bitter, and slander with no recourse. I have no problem with anyone making an honest critique of our business, we have nothing to hide. What I find distasteful is personal attacks and vile hatred from people who have nothing better to do with their time than to write cowardly poison, knowing they can hide behind half-truths. In a weird roundabout way, I would like to thank these people for helping me filter out prospective employees who have read about us online during the HR process from those who trust their own brain and what they see and hear first-hand and those that believe everything they read on the internet. It saves me a lot of time in the long run.

I do hope in the coming years that companies have the opportunity to properly challenge reviews and ask candidates to prove sweeping statements before they are allowed to post on the website. Roll on proper AI!

I think employees sometimes forget that this is a business, not a charity. All of our targets and goals go up, and often colleagues want a pay raise for doing the same job (and in many cases a worse job), and expect everything to be like Goldilocks' porridge – "juuust right". In life, we all have to work harder to stand still, because we find that the businesses we work with want more too. Travel companies want more, printers want more, paper merchants want more, and the tax man is always finding new stealth taxes to hit businesses.

It's funny, at the time of writing, a series of really personal attacks were posted online and what happened next left me in tears with a sense of happiness. My teams all over the world took to their social media accounts in disgust. One young lady sent me a beautiful letter, saying she felt like her father had been attacked and that she appreciated everything I did for her and her colleagues.

That stupid review really backfired and it was even better when Glassdoor removed it after we pointed out the obvious lies. Whatever it says online, I will keep investing in making my people better – that is, the ones who want to get better. I will keep making Ink a great place to work and as long as my name is above the door, I will continue to leave people better than I find them. These internet trolls will not stand in the way of the truth. And the truth is, selling is bloody hard and not for everybody. But I say, let people make their own mind up based on their own experiences – and maybe they will find that they are more cut out for sales.

You will always have haters and critics. Anyone doing well gets attacked, even by people they love. You are working too hard, you don't spend enough time at home. Negativity will never go away, I repeat, never go away. As long as you understand that, you can deal with it. They don't build statues of critics. As I said earlier, other people's opinions are not important, it's what is in your heart that matters most.

Take F'in Action

Don't ignore negative reviews from customers or ex-employees. Look at your processes and see if anything can be improved. If not, reach out and suggest you contact them privately. The lessons to be learned from those who have left your company are just as important as those from the people who have joined.

18

UNDERSTAND YOUR MOTIVATION AND WHY

WHY DO YOU even come to work, I was once asked. This was a question someone asked me at seventeen years old and it's quite funny reflecting on it today. I couldn't really answer the question, I needed the money, I guess.

Today, my motivation is to make others better, my motivation is not about me. I know if I do the right thing by my people, my life will just continue to improve. I love what I do, I love my teams when they succeed and when they fail.

Remember these words, you don't need to be sick to get better. We all have the gene in us to be amazing at what we do. As long as you don't put limits on yourself, you can and will achieve anything you want. Anyone working for me receives a 100% guarantee I will do whatever I can to make them the best version of themselves. It's a two-way street. They have to want to come along for the ride, and I have so many success stories to prove it.

I regularly get notes from ex-employees thanking me. Some of them left unhappy but realised with time that I was doing the right thing by them. I am sometimes aggressive in my delivery and some of my leadership team crave recognition from me – it's always tough to get. I want people to get better, they don't get better by being told how great they are all the time. That creates the wrong energy. We all need to work out the right exchange rate for feedback. How much do you have to give in order for me to give you the praise you require? Just like the pound/dollar rate it will fluctuate. Until you know what is a fair exchange rate, whatever you do will not be enough.

One of the stories I recite to people is the story of the Welsh goalkeeper, probably one of the greatest goalkeepers of the Eighties. And at the end of his career, he said to his boss, "Boss, why did you never compliment me? Even when the TV and the papers said I was Man of the Match, you would always find a couple of things I did wrong. Was it so hard to say well done?"

And the answer was a beaut! He said, "Had I done that, you would have never been as good a player as you were. You worked harder every week and every week you got better and better."

Managing people is one of the toughest things to

do. I do not know who will turn up each day, I don't know if they have had a good or bad journey in, or if they may have had an argument with their partner – and that's before they pick up the phone and have to deal with the challenges of the job. My teams come from different backgrounds, different upbringings, different countries with different core beliefs, yet we make things work, we share a common belief and they know that my desire for their lives to get better and live the life of their dreams is what motivates me every day.

It sounds all a bit Mills and Boon and I promise you my leadership skills and motivation growing up were driven by success and money. I just wanted to be rich and by twenty-one, I had a house in one the nicest areas in London, drove a Daimler, and partied with film stars. Yes, it was nice but it didn't last. I remember sending the keys back to the mortgage company being one of the low points in my life.

The other low point was when I started out in media, my now-wife paid for our first holiday together, as I could not afford to take us away. We went to Malta, it was freezing and we shared a room with a family of cockroaches. I promised her that day that she would never pay for a holiday again and we would only go to nice places. For the past twenty years, I have kept my word and every year our holidays get bigger and more exciting. Next summer, we are heading back to Malta. This time it's five-star all the way.

I spent a lot of time after my fortieth birthday really attempting to understand myself. I had four kids, a beautiful wife, a good business, yet I was really unhappy. I went on a happiness quest and spent a year reading, watching, and going to everything that was connected to happiness and learned much about myself. I went to study at Harvard as I thought I missed out on education and realised that I hadn't. What I had learned through the university of life had left me in good stead. I am good at negotiating, I am sharp of mind, and I'm able to mix well with whoever I meet.

The year culminated with me asking the business to put together a Happinkness book. It was like pulling teeth, but we got there in the end, they thought I was on some hippy mission. That piece of work won so many awards for internal communications and set the tone for the culture piece of the business. For the past ten years, we've produced a book every year that shares all the amazing things we have done as a business. They are a great reminder for everyone that as a business it's all about our people.

Building a business, I did neglect a lot of being at home and being a great dad. I am so proud of how my boys have grown up, their understanding and value of money, and their desire to work and earn their own money. They all have my traits, gawd help 'em.

Over the last couple of years, I've refused to miss football games or important occasions. We have tremendous holidays together, even if some describe me as a Disneyland dad. Our time away and the time we spend together allows me to help them get better. They've watched as I put myself through so many challenges in my life and I think deep down this has created determination in them to get better and better themselves.

And my long-suffering wife – five boys, huge amounts of testosterone, dirty pants, farting, burping, and foul language and that's just the morning before school. She has been the rock that holds us all together, without her support and commitment, most of what we have achieved would not be possible. Despite being married twenty-one years, the last eleven have been incredible – not that the first ten were not, they were tough and I needed luck each time a child was born to get through that year.

My family are my motivation, I had no idea how life would end up but all I know is I have never, for one second, stopped in my desire to give them the most incredible years of their lives. I will continue to work hard and make sure I do what I can to make everyone's lives better.

You need to find your thing, the thing that ensures you do the hard things even when you don't feel like it. You need to make sure you give attention to the most important things. If you find yourself abusing your attention, life starts disintegrating very quickly.

You must have the will to fight, you have to have the dedication to your craft and the determination to succeed in spite of every situation, market condition, or political woes.

Over the years, we picked up people with no experience and others who were down on their luck and turned them into heroes and helped them create the most amazing lives. Actually, we hired those no one else believed in. We believed in them and went to work to make them better than we found them. We didn't always succeed and sometimes people were vicious about us. But in the end, we learned to conquer diversity together, as a family.

Take F'in Action

Give as much positive energy to your business as you do your family. You'll never get an equal balance all the time, but neither deserves to get less of you because the other is taking up too much. Find ways to treat your employees both as individuals and as a team when it comes to praise and helping them develop.

19

THE CHALLENGES

THE SECOND DAY was about to begin: we were about to embark on 26.2 miles across the Sahara. I was in the most amount of pain I had ever experienced. We'd already walked a marathon across the desert, it was 100°F and I had blisters on blisters. The medics recommended I didn't continue. I told them that there was no way I would not be leading these guys across the finish line.

One more marathon to go. It was like walking on broken glass, no skin on my feet, bloody toes and pain that felt like being stabbed every footstep. It became a mental battle, every pitstop I would change socks and even shoes. I was swallowing pain killers like sweets and knocking back Red Bull and Haribo to keep going. By the time we arrived at the finish line, I sprinted – and I mean sprinted – for the finish. No one could understand how I got across that line. I lost all my toenails, I had to have my feet shaved and

, but it was all worth it.

ey for the Royal National pital Charity and I was lucky HRH Princess Eugenie and get a very ou from her for our achievements. This eve ow a regular on our calendar each year, with ten Inkers crossing the Sahara to raise money for charity – we have raised over £40,000 since we started and I'm glad to say no one has had to endure what I went through.

As a prelude to the Sahara walk, we took on the London to Brighton 100km walk – how difficult could that be? Well, when your wife throws out your faithful walking boots (she maintains, rightly, that I should have checked my kit earlier than the night before), the weather turns into a monsoon, and most of it is through muddy fields, it becomes a nightmare. I probably should not have stopped at the chip shop after just 5 miles. But hey ho, I was hungry.

In the end, about twenty-five of us started and only eight finished. I got to about 60km before the blisters became too much of an issue. All those who finished were mentally tarnished, and in a bad way. It was one day-through-the-night adventure and having done so many events, this was tougher than anything I had done before, or even did after. I was so disappointed that I let down my colleagues by not finishing. That's the reason I refused to give up on the Sahara. And I did thoroughly check all my equipment before I left this time, including buying new walking boots!

Rewind to 2006, and I was being encouraged by my colleagues to do a 10k run. "I don't do running," I said. They pushed and convinced me and I began to train. I could not get to the end of the road before I ran out of puff but that did not deter me. Halfway through the training, I said, "If I do this 10k, I'm going to do a whole marathon." In the UK, Snicker bars were once called Marathons and most of my friends thought I was talking about the chocolate bar.

The financial crisis has just started and doom and gloom was everywhere. I used the fact that I would run a marathon as an example that anything is possible. If I could do this, with my weight and condition, selling a few ads would be a doddle. From that day onwards, I trained and ran and ran. I ran ten half marathons, the New York Marathon, and then the double marathon across the Sahara.

Then, I got bored of just running and turned my attention to triathlons. And soon enough I did my first little one, then a half Olympic, and then an Olympic. It was only right to test myself and go for the Ironman, well, half – 1.2-miles swim, 90km bike, and a half marathon. After 8 hours 33 minutes I finished – the last to finish, 726th (which wasn't that bad as over a thousand had started). It was so tough, so many had dropped out but I seemed to have a police escort the whole way and somehow I kept going.

In 2012, I wanted to push us a little bit harder so Michael and I took eight people and we decided to summit Kilimanjaro. This was a walk in the park for the first five days and then on summit night the challenge became real: it was freezing and painful. I wanted to stop more than a dozen times, those Haribo and Red Bull came out again. My guide was my guardian angel – he would not let me stop. While the others summited early and didn't get much time at the top, I didn't reach it until the sun had come out and it was already quite warm. As a result, I had a long time up there along with businessman and author Chet Holmes' daughter Amanda. Chet had long been an inspiration for me and had sadly just died so I was pleased to be able to share that moment with her.

As I stood on top of the mountain, I thought to myself, "What's next?" I could never really enjoy experiences, I was always interested in what to do next. Funnily enough, since the Sahara that emotion has gone Other than playing football at Wembley,

Anfield or the Emirates, my challenges are behind me, well, sort of... I am now on a mission to skydive, but I need to lose three stone, which is what I am determined to do.

I think the reason I kept doing these challenges was to prove to me and others, including my sons, that anything is possible. That there is nothing in life you cannot do if you put your mind to it. It helped me get through 2008-13, which were some of the toughest years modern businesses had ever experienced. It gave all the teams a physical and concrete way of showing that you can achieve anything if you put your mind to it.

Challenges make for the greatest stories. It's so important to remember your words are powerful, your thoughts are the direction of your travel. Speak and think kindly and the journey will be a hell of a lot better. With so many things to worry about, it's amazing we get anything done. Be kind with your thinking, where you spend your time and who with.

For me, life has been challenging and good in equal measures. It is the encounters that you speak of when you want to motivate others. It is your past trials that give you strength when you face new ones. Although I love the success, it is the challenge that makes the greatest story.

Take F'in Action

Use this book as inspiration – if I can do it, you can too. Consider if you need to change who you spend your time with and who is influencing and positively affecting you.

20

GETTING BETTER

HOW DO I GET BETTER? This was a question I constantly asked myself. After all, I wasn't prepared to stagnate. I kept reading, I went to personal growth seminars, I did four executive education courses at the biggest universities on the planet, I studied everything relevant. I even qualified in hypnosis, passed exams in how to analyse handwriting and learnt all about mindfulness and negotiating.

All of these skills have helped me improve my ability to interact with anyone I meet. I understand the use of language, I speak a little bit of about twenty languages; enough to ask how people are or at least say good morning. I learned to be less judgemental and not to have to win every battle, I even learned to say sorry sometimes. I am on a journey to become a better version of myself, and this is a never-ending conveyor belt.

I realised a few simple things: for anything to get better I had to get better. I had to do more and the more I did, the better things would get. Do more, get better. If I found moments when I was struggling, I would reach out and find someone who could give me the answer I needed. And as things changed and improved, I would adjust my thinking to that change. It really was that simple. Take a lot of personal responsibility and constant, never-ending improvement.

I made it clear to everyone around me that our job was to make everyone around us better, and as long as we stuck to that principle, all our lives would improve. Whilst it seems like an easy concept, it takes a bloody long time and people run out of patience. Today, I am now a long-game player. I don't care about the short-term thinking or results, I am interested in making people great for a long time to come. As some of the chapters have proved, youngsters today need an instant fix, they want instant gratification and when they don't get it, they revolt, bitch, moan, and blame anyone close to them for their failing.

I have stopped blaming or looking for someone to blame so I can feel better about myself (apart from my wife throwing away my hiking boots). Take personal responsibility for everything that happens to you. It's your fault, whatever happens, nobody else's.

Life is about adding value to others. If you only

focus on the money, you will never have enough. Every year, some people work so much harder than others and get very little in return; and there are others who didn't work as hard and made a lot more money – life is not fair.

Look in the mirror every day, do you like what you see? Spend time at the end of each day thinking about what went well and what you are grateful for. Tell people who matter that you do appreciate and care about them. Little acts of kindness do go a very long way. As I write this, I realise I have a lot more work to do to get better.

Here's another way to think about this: if you had everything you ever wanted but you were the only person left on Earth, would you still want it?

Take F-in Action

Learn to like yourself because it's much easier to work on success when you're not in self-doubt mode. If there is something you don't like, either work on improving it or embrace it and move on. Set annual development goals – do a course each year, try something new, give yourself a reading challenge.

21

WHO IS THE SALESPERSON?

OVER THE YEARS so many salespeople have walked through our doors. They have been a mix, from over-enthusiastic puppies to the hardened, weathered sales heroes. Many are pretty selfish, shallow, self-centred know-it-alls; been there done that, got the t-shirt (and even met the guy who made it).

Despite making all the right noises, it's really hard to find enough people with the work ethic and the desire to practise and master our trade. What we do is bloody tough. Even when they are committed, the barrage of 'NO' wears them down. Too many find it way too hard, they forget very quickly what they promised in the interview and all the talk takes a sharpish walk. If you want to sell for a living it really takes a lot of strength of character. I think you need to be slightly odd and have a love of pain and suffering that comes with constant objections as well as an unfaltering resilience and faith.

There's such a fine line between the rockstar and rock bottom. A couple of bad days and suddenly everything is a disaster. Ringing the bell for the first time to announce that deal to the office can be better than any high – better than sex, some say. And once you get the bug, it's a hard profession to turn away from.

When our salespeople have been paid, they relax, which is a big mistake; and when they are pawning the watch to get through the month, they suddenly focus and relight the fire. In the 'dog eat dog world' of sales it takes real guts to last – yesterday's deal is forgotten in a heartbeat. You have to keep proving your worth and are only as good as the next deal on the table.

As our business got stronger, I wanted to remove this feeling. I didn't want people to worry about money or job safety as long as they came in and did an honest day's work.

In my early days of sales, I saw people fired on the spot at morning meetings. No warnings, no disciplinary, just get the fuck out and never darken our door again. The world was a rough and tough place back then. Today, we give people so many chances before we give up on them. We work hard to make them as good as we can. Sometimes, we have given people more chances than we should and it always comes back to bite us on the arse. I've learned to trust my gut instinct more.

Over the years, we have had many salespeople and sales coaches come and go. The truth is those who can sell, sell and those that can't, teach. The latter may decide to become coaches, advisors, or walk down the street giving others life advice. On one day recently, I watched three ex-employees (who quit because they could not even sell or, worse still, didn't like the dirty process of selling) giving out advice on how to be great salespeople and how to be great in life.

These are people who struggled to get out of bed on most days, who had the backbone and determination of a snail. Social media now gives them an audience of people needing reassurance that everything will be OK. In life, there are way too many people giving advice, yet not living it themselves. These people are often living unhappy lives, in unhappy relationships, and yet painting a picture of happiness and magical joy.

My guidance to you, whoever you take advice from, is this: make sure they have the aptitude to practise what they preach. Otherwise, you end up taking advice on how to make the perfect life from people who are only good at the sales pitch or, worse still, they are pretenders. Listen to people who have the stamina to really survive and thrive.

If you want to make a career in sales it's not about how talented you are, it's about how big the fire in your belly is and how resilient and ambitious you are. It's a profession where less talent and more tenaciousness pays very well.

When things start to go wrong, salespeople are the first to tell you how they used to do it better at their old company. How the way you do things around here is not the right way; they become bitter very quickly. It's funny over time, when they look back, we were actually good for them and their career. I have yet to see anyone who left early in the process go on and make themselves amazing. I have seen a lot fail. And the majority are still jumping from company to company looking for perfection. It's never the company, it's always about you, so if you find yourself making excuses for why you are not selling as much as the guy on the next desk, just stop and be honest with yourself.

Great salespeople make average employers great. Salespeople are not naturally a generous bunch, giving anything is alien.

Nearly every salesperson I have ever met, has a scarcity mindset and think however well they are doing, it will stop at any minute. Most salespeople have a terrible relationship with money, it really does scare them: they fritter it, gamble it, drink it, spend far too much on recreational drugs, and waste the rest. I believe it's a dripping tap that will run and run. There truly is more money available today than at any time in history. I spend my energy turning people from being scared of money, to spending, giving it away, being charitable and overly generous. I want them to embrace it and love it for what it is.

The energy on the sales floor is vital to its success – you need to build an energetic, exciting environment. The challenge is managing the people. Salespeople are always in search of instant gratification. Drugs and sex among salespeople are common. They think only other salespeople really understand what they are going through. Partners tell them they are working too hard, they just don't get it. They build great friendships, which last for years, real friendships with people who have been through or are going through the same head fuck as them. It's a funny phenomenon that happens in stressful professions.

In times of stress, I see it all the time, the cracks start to show. When they want to join us, they will do and say anything to get the job. It's no different to getting into a great university, it's all very exciting getting the acceptance letter with the promise of a bright future. They are pumped, ready for their journey ahead, then they realise how difficult it is in reality and they have to do so much bloody work. When it gets a bit hard, they look at who they can blame – the product doesn't work, the market is rubbish, the way you run your business is wrong, the plants you have in the office are draining my energy, and did I mention that the headsets are terrible. They turn from hero to victims and forget all the positives of working in a sales environment. The complaints come thick and fast – the incentives are stupid, the commission scheme is unfair, working environment is unbearable, the managers are bullies, there are too many micro-managers and every other criticism under the sun. Managing this is the art form.

Take F'in Action

Listen to what people are telling and showing you by their words and behaviour. If someone is failing, give them the chance to learn through coaching and training and if they won't admit they need help then they are getting in their own way. If you plan to invest time and money on coaching, then do your research.
Ask for recommendations, speak to their clients, look at their own work.

22

NO ONE UNDERSTANDS US

IN OUR COMPANY, most of our business is done by cold calling. The teams reach out and have to, in a very short period, spark the person's interest. That's not an easy thing to do.

Every day, we make sales doing just this simple thing. Take my advice, don't overcook your sales process. Selling on the phone is harder than face to face. I believe if it can be done on the phone, do it on the phone. If it can't, get on a plane, train, or whatever and go and see them in person. Nothing beats the work you can do in a day on the telephone. You have your voice to make things happen. But equally, when you sit opposite someone you have so much more in your arsenal. You can read the body language, emotion, you can judge if they are interested.

The voice and language are such powerful tools, the magic you have within you creates the life you want. When someone sells, you have money in your voice, so use it over and over. Don't waste time smoking, making tea, and celebrating. Get back on the phone.

I have spent my life drumming into salespeople that there is more work to do than can ever be done, more money to make than has ever been made. (That inspiration comes from *Circle of Life,* from *The Lion King*, by the way!) I love the law of attraction and a feeling that you can order what you want out of life. It's like ordering a pizza, you just can't guarantee a thirty-minute delivery time that's all. You have to be patient and have some faith and trust in the process – so order what you want out of life. The more positive you are, the more encouraging and helpful to others, the better life turns out for you. I believe it's really that simple.

In the early years, every time a salesperson asked me for anything, such as, "I want a pay rise/a week off," I would say, "Great. I want a Bentley." It became a running push back. For my fortieth birthday, the whole sales floor clubbed together and got me a powder blue Bentley convertible for the weekend. I loved the feeling of driving around town in this masterpiece and clearly, they really did listen.

Soon after, I had a big global sales gathering at Birkbeck University in London and I remember standing up giving the teams a talk about having whatever you want out of life. As I sat down, I thought "you hypocrite". And so, I ordered the car I wanted – a stunning black Bentley. The negotiation was simple, here's my offer, take it or leave it. It was the heart of the recession and selling luxury cars was a tad challenging. It's the only car I ever made any money on. The funniest part of the whole negotiation was asking if I could put my personal number plate on the car. He said, "Sure, what is it?" I said "CL05 ER X." He chuckled as he knew I had closed a great deal.

Although driving in a car like that is a pleasure, I actually spend most of my life at 30,000 feet – which happens to be roughly the same amount of decisions humans make every day. And so, if you constantly lie to yourself, you will soon begin to despise yourself. The key problem in our lives is that we keep letting ourselves down. And when you think about it, you are the person you spend most of your time with. If you can't be happy in your company, why should anyone else be?

During our lives, we are on a journey with ourselves; and if it feels like sitting next to the most annoying person on the plane, the journey is going to be painful. Find out who you are, what you stand for, and enjoy your company. A great test is spending a week alone, just thinking. If you can't afford to take a week to yourself for whatever reason, then find another way to do this. Perhaps set aside an hour or an afternoon regularly, without other people, social media, or any other distractions. Whatever you set on, commit to it. A good life comes from not breaking promises to yourself.

In life you must find freedom, and I'm not talking about financial freedom. You need to be able to not worry about what people might be saying or thinking about you. You need to have the confidence and self-belief to deal with everything that is thrown at you, both good and bad. The time you spend with problems needs to be short and precise. The truth is most issues rarely matter that much. Nothing is that important and the saying, "this too will pass" is invariably spot on.

If you can find that place, your life will be one that improves and excites you to live it. You really can have whatever you want in life if you remove your fear of money. I did it and every day since, I have never stopped to think, what if?

Opportunityisnowhere. You must decide how you read this. Imagine a life where you can have anything you ever wanted. This is selling for me.

Money and incentives are really important to a winning mentality. What's also very important is recognition. Salesperson of the week, month, and year are coveted titles and every year we run award ceremonies to celebrate the best of the best across the business. In 2018, we introduced a new visual celebration. The heavyweight belt for salesperson of the week. We went to a boxing belt manufacturer and got them to make us a special belt that we give out every Friday. We couple this with a picture in the weekly roundup. And at the end of the year, the person who won the most belts during the year gets a further cash bonus. The salesperson gets to keep the belt on their desk all week and earns extra commission on all their deals while they are belt holders.

It ticks every box: recognition, reward, and visual greatness. In short, the sales person's dream. It is decided each week for a combination of attitude, revenue, and helping others. That's what people need to focus on – winning, not money or material things. It's winning all the accolades you can muster, that's what makes a great long-term sales career.

Sales is a funny phenomenon. If you get good at it, you can have a better life than all those who studied and trained for years for a 'proper profession', like a doctor or lawyer. Sales is an art form – we now play in the Premier League, not the lower leagues.

Most people don't realise or know how hard it is

and I laugh at all the people who criticise us. I also love anyone that says, "I did sales when I was deciding what I wanted to do in life," or "I did sales when I was in college." They don't realise that life is sales and sales is life.

You must never forget, salespeople are real people and they get upset easily, they get down quickly, and they can lose belief way too much. You need to know them inside and out. What makes them tick, what pisses them off (and use that), what inspires them, and what will light the fuse to make them perform. Being a great sales leader is also an art form: they don't need to like you, they just need to see themselves getting better.

The craft is understanding how to blend it all – when to kick, when to push, when to pull. You see it a lot today with footballers, highly paid prima donnas, who have given up the love of just playing football for money. When is the moment we stop loving what we do and will only do it for whoever will pay us the highest amount of money?

It's quite sad really and shows very little loyalty to those who make you better than you were. If you don't do things that motivate, inspire, reward and keep doing it daily, the pressure gets too much and people quit, get down in dumps, or worse.

Remember to use the phrase, "I get to", rather than "I have to". It's this language transference that makes a big difference to our interpretations. I get to go to work, I get to work hard, and I get to learn more. Never convince yourself that you don't have everything that you need to be brilliant. You have all the skills, it's just that some of them remain dormant until you ignite them.

If you are looking for a magic formula, then this is it. It's a combination of hard work, persistence, and perspiration. The top tier of salespeople who have worked out the formula are the best ones to make you incredible. The leaders who make their people better are the ones you need to gravitate towards.

Find the best, stick to them and learn from them. It's ridiculously simple but people think they might get rejected if they ask for help. They won't. Anyone who is any good will help others, they love competition, they love challenges, and want as much of it as possible, and they are also bright enough to realise that if the company does well, so do they. If the company doesn't, their own business is at risk.

Take F'in Action

Every time you get to the point in your life and business where you have hit a certain milestone, reward yourself with the thing you said you would have. "If I can earn enough in a four-day week, then I'm going to do it." "If I become a millionaire, I'll buy a yacht." The best tip I can give you is spend the most time you can with whoever is doing it best at your company.

23

THERE REALLY WAS NO F IN SALES

IMAGINE HUNDREDS OF salespeople. That's a lot of overhead – salaries, phones, expenses, rent, rates – and then imagine that business dries up. That's what happened after 9/11 and again in 2008/9 and 2012. How do you change that mindset when no one is selling? You talk to your competitors and they tell you it's tough. You have two options: you agree to participate in the pity party or you get up and fight back.

Let's start with 9/11. I was having lunch with a big watch advertiser at the Ritz. You never forget where you were when tragedies happen. I was in Beirut when Princess Diana died and that was a shocking day filled with conspiracy theories and disbelief. Yet, while everyone was still reeling from the shock and implications of 9/11, our business was stable by December that year. It had been a tough couple of months but in that period we won a major low-cost airline contract and business was back to normal.

The airline had been through six publishers since they started. People told me I was mad taking on this fledgling airline. I remember the publisher for British Airways telling one of my team that this will kill us off once and for all. Today, eighteen years later, it's the biggest airline in the UK and one of the largest in the world. We have grown with them and today sell so many of their marketing assets. We were brave. Our attitude was simple: if they fill the planes, we will find advertisers. And I was right, the airline sold the seats and we found the right brands to advertise, from just twelve destinations back then. Today, we sell thousands of adverts every month in hundreds of markets across the world, some in places you have never even heard of. We still do it the same way, by picking up the phone or, if we have to, jumping on a plane somewhere. Was it inexperienced mindless belief, was it a determination to succeed, or just luck? I think a combination of all three.

In 2005, I was in New York and had a meeting with an exec from one of the sales companies who were selling the US market into Europe. He said the market for them had not recovered yet. I was flabbergasted as I wandered down Fifth Avenue trying to make sense of what I'd been told. We were clearly doing something right.

People and companies blame situations and circumstances when things don't go well or they just don't have a great business plan. My friend works for Cantor Fitzgerald, their HQ was on the 101st floor of the World Trade Center and in the 9/11 attack lost nearly 70% of their workforce. They were really affected by 9/11, yet they still remain in business today. Another friend ran a business in Brisbane Australia, which is so far away from NY, yet he blamed the attacks for the failure of his business. How can this be true or make any sense? Businesses fail or succeed because of the 78% rule; because they are not robust enough or the owners are not committed enough, not because outside forces get in the way. Everything else is just excuses.

This was a wake-up call for what would follow. We had SARS, we had ash clouds in Europe, and then along came the big one in 2008. Don't turn on the TV I would say, there is nothing positive to come out of this. Our advertisers are going bust, no one can pay their bills. This was a dark time for selling. Yet, the principles of 9/11 remained, the planes were still full, people who wanted to steal market share were being opportunistic. In this time, new brands were formed. This is actually where real growth happened. I said to my teams, the world is not in a great place, we are in a recession but we are not taking part. I started doing things that were physically tough to prove to the teams what was possible and I got to work to instil a sense of belief in all our people.

Throughout 2007-12, we didn't lose money. We worked harder than everyone else I knew in the media industry. Most seemed to have given up, but we didn't. I went on an aggressive recruitment drive – while others were laying off, I would be hiring. It actually became a really good time and when the market came back, we were in pole position to take advantage. We didn't sit on our arses waiting for the phone to ring, we got on planes and went and turned over so many stones, we found businesses who were doing well and showed them how they could take advantage of the turmoil. Many of those businesses still promote with us today.

We helped businesses grow. In every market place, there are winners and whingers. You just need to decide how committed you and your teams are. We had many a panic board meeting and we cut lots of our cloth accordingly, but we didn't cut people, we held on as much as we could and invested in them to help them deal with quite a big cut to earning potential. The only thing we had in our favour is that we had customers flying every day, we had a guaranteed audience that everyone else was struggling to find. I also knew that the industry was in turmoil, where were they going to go?

In 2010, European countries started to go bust, first Ireland, Iceland, Portugal and then Greece. Unemployment in Europe reached its highest ever levels, the markets were a clusterfuck. Spain was teetering on the brink and then the ECB found a way to calm things down in 2012.

That was nearly a five-year period when on more days than not we had no F'in sales. I had belief though. I used the physical challenges and positive messages to get me and my teams through with an insane belief that we would win. We were lucky as we were never limited to one market, as one market softened and one sector struggled, we changed direction.

I was also lucky in 2000. We had never had much success selling to the dot.com sector, so when the bubble burst, we were fairly protected. However, in 2008, when the real estate market crumbled, we had a lot of eggs in that basket. Florida, Spain, France, and Portugal used to give us thirty pages a month – overnight that disappeared. We were agile and nimble and found new revenue streams, though. We found money that no one else was looking for.

From about 2009, the world kept predicting the

end of print. "Print is dead" the headlines would read. When 100% of your revenues come from print, you need to consider this carefully. Yet, in 2019, some ten years on, we sell more print pages than ever, the market remains bullish and I don't see it slowing for many years. As a business, we will deliver content in whatever format people want to consume it in. No one yet has devised a better ephemeral experience than a good old-fashioned magazine. And digitisation within the cabin is still not getting much traction.

We survived the iPad that was going to kill us and the smartphone too. They are great devices, but don't give the lean-back experience of reading a magazine nor the inspiration that comes from a glossy picture or in-depth article. There's something uniquely relaxing, even hypnotic about flicking through the crisp pages of a magazine – resting your eyes from the flickering white light of technology – it's a mindful experience and one which can't be replicated by a screen.

There may be alternatives to print, but there are alternatives to many things in life. We haven't stopped using ships because planes were invented – they both may take you to the same place but it's a very different experience going on a cruise to boarding an Airbus. Whatever doesn't kill you makes you stronger, right?

It certainly does. Today, the business is stronger than ever; the belief and mindset are tremendous and it's all down to the belief of the people that work here. "We sell every day" is our mantra. There are lots of F'in sales and no matter what comes next we are ready.

If I believe the media hype as I type this, then we are heading for a recession; and let's be honest, the media have predicted twenty-seven of the last two recessions. There is no reason for the world to come to an end unless people keep talking it down, keep fighting free trade and become too protectionist. I don't know what will happen with Brexit, but in the UK we will be just fine.

Take F'in Action

Just because your industry is struggling or someone tells you it's dead, doesn't make it true. But you need a strategy. Don't just dig your heels in because it's your company. Know when to fold and when to raise. There is a saying, "Build it, and they will come." In business, unfortunately, it's rarely true. Business will not come knocking on your door, so go out and find it, ask for help, support your teams, and grow your business.

24

THE NEW NORMAL

DURING THE TOUGH times of 2008, I came up with my new normal, a new way of doing things. This really did mess with some people's minds. Too many were stuck in their ways of doing things and my new format didn't go down that well.

I met a courageous lady who lost both her legs in the 7/7 attack in London and she told me that she had no hatred for the bombers. She was the most beautiful human I had ever met. She could no longer bounce down the stairs, so she had to create a new normal. We had not suffered, we were just finding doing business a little tougher, but creating our new normal practices helped us get things back on track. We stopped allowing ourselves to lie to ourselves. We held each accountable to the promises and commitments we made to each other. We were hard on each other otherwise we would have slipped back.

It truly was a tough time and that's when in order to survive you need to think differently. If you lie to us, that's not ideal but the concept of lying to yourself was the one we really focused on eliminating. We made shit happen, while others looked at what and who they could blame.

One of my biggest frustrations is how many of my team overthink everything. They procrastinate so much that they end up doing nothing. Stop overthinking and start doing! Make the mistakes and learn. Sitting on the fence only does one thing, it gives you a sore bum. During this time, I asked myself the question, do I love to win or hate to lose?

I came to the realisation that I love to win and I love to lose. I learnt so much from my losses and they made me stronger and more determined to come back for some more. So many people are waiting for me to fail, that's the reason I keep winning and keep going every day.

Take F'in Action

What actions can you put in place to prevent overthinking? Can you create a process to be followed after every loss so that the focus is on learning a lesson and moving on? There are going to be days you struggle and procrastinate. Find people to inspire you, read their stories, watch their YouTube videos, buy their books. There are people who are dealing with all kinds of problems and we can learn from one another.

25

LIMITLESS AND THE REVOLUTION

TWO THINGS THAT really helped us change our mindset were The Revolution we put together in 2012 and Limitless Thinking in 2018. We wanted to do something very different. We were radical and decided to reward people on behaviour rather than sales. It was an interesting experiment, most of my top salespeople decided to quit. They didn't like the fact they were not being rewarded on their results.

In some instances, we paid commission to salespeople who did no business, but showed the right attitude. It was our job to coach them to get the sales coming in. This whole system put the power back into the leadership team to manage their people more effectively. It created many headaches and arguments but in a short period of time, we changed some of the culture from greed to doing the right things daily. It was a huge shift in the industry and many of my competitors rubbed their hands with glee, mopping up some of my big hitters.

The thing they all missed was that these guys were only big hitters because of our environment, our unique sales floor and culture. Take an animal out of the wild, stick 'em in a zoo and they behave the same as the others in the zoo. There was no energetic sales environment like the one we had created. We kept strong for about a year before we made some adjustments. Today, we still reward new people based on this method. Their commission is based on work rate and work ethic. Once they have experience, we move them on to a yield-based scheme. Looking back, it was a time to be brave and while some bits of it worked, some left too much to interpretation with a young forming leadership team.

Energy on the sales floor is what makes our salespeople great. That's why we have energy sessions every morning. Some people don't like these either, especially some of the more mature ones. However, it wakes us up from a terrible journey in and gets us fired up to take on the day.

Over the years, I have had my best salespeople move home or country and want to continue working from home – it has never worked. The energy in the office is infectious, the ideas and inspiration come from a dynamic sales floor which just can't be replicated elsewhere. Our sales floor adds 50-75% better performance, especially when the music is blaring and the noise is infectious.

In 2018, we introduced the Limitless mindset with a new performance coach and went about instilling this into the sales floor. Being limitless means that anything and everything is possible and we went about driving our people to achieve amazing feats both in and out of work. I am so proud and pleased with the results and change in behaviours.

So many records have been smashed and salespeople are doing bigger, longer, and higher value deals. We broke through the ceilings and limits people had got used to. What was once a £65,000 a month salesperson was now doing over £100,000 and doing it every month. New language, new belief patterns, and a whole new earning capacity. Not necessarily selling much more space, just valuing their assets better.

Limitless is a great word, it creates a whole new mindset of what is possible. Some of the shift in performance blew our minds – 200-300% growth in a matter of months.

It's funny now looking back on The Revolution. At the time it took quite a lot of balls to do it and we definitely learned a hell of a lot by going through the process. It goes to show that you don't need to follow the herd, rather create your own economy and rules. And no matter if it goes well or badly, it's better to experiment and learn than to keep doing the same thing and expect different results.

Take F'in Action

Look at what you did on the mornings and evenings of your very best days. Can you see a pattern? Your first actions of the day and your final thoughts and emotions before you go to sleep are important. Be brave – just because something is working well, doesn't mean that things should stay the same. Change is vital to growth.

26

WEIGHT LOSS

WITH ALL THE exciting changes and success of the business, there is still one elusive goal. The only challenging part of my personal life. My inability to lose weight and keep it off. Over the years, I've lost as much as six stone. Sadly, I put weight back on.

I remain at 300lbs today, even with a healthy regime and a goodish diet. This is not a pity plea chapter. I know I eat too much, I clearly love eating more than I want to lose weight. But I want to share what I put myself through, what worked, and what I enjoyed. The noise that reverberates in my brain is that I have so many people relying on me and four boys and wife that need me. One coach said to me, without you around, the world would be a worse place for so many. This one thing frustrates me the most.

You know the worst day to start dieting? Any day. Diets are what we give animals. The whole notion of a diet is wrong; it's a lifestyle and I have not found the right one yet.

Let's start at sixteen years old. My dad took me to the Henlow Grange Health Farm for the first time. After a week I lost some weight and felt great – this put me on the road to thinking about my health and well-being. Over the years, I have become a regular at health farms. They give me a place to go to kick-start my routine, they just don't seem to help me maintain it.

I experimented all along my weight loss journey. The first weird thing I did was going to the Karlovy Vary in the Czech Republic. I was hosed down by some weird people in white coats. I was living on broth and boiled potatoes for a week. The town has numerous thermal springs and the water there was able to fix most things. I was put through a vigorous Eastern European experience. No one spoke much English and communicating was fun. I felt cleansed.

Today, I can get a similar experience at the Russian Spa room on Collins Avenue in Miami. I love the ridiculous hot shvitz, but it's the ice-cold baths that make me feel alive.

Juice fasting was the next cool thing I found. I went off to Moinhos Velhos in the Algarve. This was going back to nature (even the mobile phone didn't work there). At the beginning of the week, I was stressed and toxic, by the end of it I felt like I had been cleansed inside and out, like I had been put through a fast cycle on the washing machine. My eyes were clear, my skin was tingling, and I felt alive. A daily routine of fresh juice and vegetable broth, yoga and self-induced colonics. Despite having no food, I had more energy than at any time in my adult life. I really should have done this more often. Again, when I am in Miami these days, I have a colonic and love the juice bars.

I had success with Lighter Life – it was basically milkshakes for breakfast, lunch, and dinner. I lost so much weight people didn't recognise me. In eleven weeks I had shed 6 stone (84lbs). I had a new wardrobe and felt amazing. I was never going back to be fat again. Wrong, I loved food too much, so as soon as I started eating normally again the willpower subsided and there I was enjoying the odd bag of chips and doughnuts. Why, oh why, after such success, did I self-sabotage? I can't answer that. I wish I understood it.

More recently, I spent a week in Red Mountain in Utah, where I found my mojo again. I trained well, ate well, and the environment allowed me to rebalance. They sent me to the local hospital and put me through every test known to mankind. At the end of it, my cholesterol was one of the lowest the doctor had ever seen. I was overweight, actually obese, yet my fitness levels were good. I asked the doctor why I was not losing weight, and her answer horrified me. It's probably genetic, she said. But I know the answers lie with me.

Before my fiftieth birthday, I was determined to shed some weight. I found a great coach to help me and he recommended I buy my food from Detox Kitchen – 1200 calories delivered every day with all meals and snacks prepared. In three months, I shed 3 stone (42lbs), yet once again it was not sustainable. I found it boring. As I said at the beginning of the book, I'm not compliant, I can't follow regimes. I love freedom and I love hummus more.

I am determined as I write this to shed the weight. I take full responsibility for my situation. I am not a victim, I just need to find the right model for me that is sustainable, that allows me to enjoy my love of food and my love of getting fit. It feels a little weird. Everything else in life I seem to have mastered. This one thing still frustrates me.

I'm not lazy, I'm not undetermined, I just need to find the key. I will look after myself and I will achieve this milestone too. Maybe the process of writing this down will get me there. If you ever meet me or wanna reach out to me, kick me hard and make me drop the bag of doughnuts.

One of my goals in the next couple of years

is to create a combination of all the above in a long weekend retreat for overweight, stressed out businessmen, where I bring in the best in the world for intimate get-togethers, to talk about sleep, diet, mental toughness, and healthy regimes, and ensure everyone leaves so much better than they arrived.

Take F'in Action

If you have had a long-term goal that hasn't worked out yet, don't give up. There are many paths to success and new innovations arrive all the time, so until you try them all, you can't admit defeat. Your health and mental well-being are of the utmost importance. In my industry, stress and burnout is rife. So, take holidays, make time to relax and for loved ones, and have hobbies you enjoy. Check in with those who care about you and do the same for them.

27

DO THE RIGHT THING

SOMETIMES DOING THE right thing goes against logical or commercial behaviour. You invest in people and even if, at times, some people might disappoint or let you down, the aim of the game is to always do right by anyone you employ. We make a commitment at the interview stage and we do our best to honour our words.

All humans have issues; sometimes they want help fixing those issues, sometimes they just want someone to listen to them. I am a big believer in being there for my teams. I do get things wrong, but more times I do get things very right. And I think it's really important that you treat people the way you would like to be treated.

A few years ago, my long-time colleague in the US got extremely sick with an unknown virus, and all of a sudden deteriorated. The doctors didn't know what he had and although the team at Emory Hospital in Atlanta were fantastic, they were fighting to save his life. His wife called me and said he was in a coma and things were not looking good.

I jumped on a plane and rushed to the hospital to see him. His mother and wife had been sat by his side for days with no reaction. As I walked in and spoke my greetings his face lit up and he smiled. He then scared us all by being violently sick and choking – we joke now that it was the sight of me that made him vomit so profusely, but clearly I gave him the impetus he needed to come back fighting to this world.

Over the next seven months he slowly got better and today is back to full health, even though no one is exactly sure what caused what he had. In between times, I would fly into Atlanta on a Monday morning and get the Friday night flight home, to keep the US operation ticking over. I did this for many months, as well as my own job, managing both the office and operations in the US.

Ink supported him and his family the best we could. He had been a great servant to the business, he had helped me put the cult into the culture and it was just the right thing to do to pull out all the stops to hold the fort for him until he was well enough to return to work.

I am constantly reinforcing to my teams that living a fulfilled life is about doing the right things on as many days as you can. And if your heart is in the right place, even if you are being strict or stern, you always put your people first. Finding good, loyal teammates is hard.

This was not a one-off, we always do our best to allow people to have flexibility where we can and it doesn't affect the balance of the business but enriches it. I watched love bloom as one of my production team had a partner in Italy and we let her regularly work from there.

We are very supportive when it comes to health – not only personal, but also within the extended family. I believe we are a flexible and supportive business. This ethos runs through the company with my whole leadership team tasked with being close to their people.

Understanding what makes them tick, what drives them and how to make them better builds the relationship and creates a winning dynamic. I encourage my leadership team to support them when things are not going to plan and I am so proud and pleased at how many times they report doing the right thing in their feedback. In a high-performance business, many ignore the softer skills, emotional intelligence, in the pursuit of hitting the goal.

We are, first and foremost, a people business and

without them, it's just a few contracts and some old computers. The hardest thing to deal with is when people let you down in the process of helping them. As I have said many times in this book, there is nothing as surprising as people. Inevitably, this does happen from time to time, and I tell my management teams they shouldn't let one moment deter them from the path that we as a business have chosen to walk down.

I know from experience that everything happens for a reason and if it's not clear to us now why that person behaved in a certain way maybe it will be in the future. Perhaps we will hear from them in years to come when they are older and wiser. Or maybe they will just be the one that got away. But one thing is sure, even if we bear a few disappointments, it in no way dulls the shine of the many, many times we know we acted in the best ways we could. We hold our heads up high and carry on, and leave karma to sort the rest.

Take F'in Action

Your employees have pain points, just the same as your customers. Often, we only find them out after they have quit. Invest time in building a rapport with your key people and ensure they have a good relationship and open communication with their teams. It is your job to steer the ship and when things go in an unexpected or negative direction, you need to take responsibility and set an example for your people.

28

TIME IN COURT

OVER ALL THESE YEARS I have had a few challenging issues. I don't believe in suing people, karma has its way of working things out. However, on a few occasions, people took me to task. One win and three defeats tell you it's not a great place to be.

My first visit to the High Court was to defend an injunction that was issued to stop me publishing a title called *Entrée*. It was a restaurant magazine I produced to go with my free magazine. One of my competitors had a similar product and tried to stop me from printing. I took a barrister and went to battle – going to court is just like selling, the best story wins. I had also done a lot of homework, which is something I think all good salespeople need to do. I had got permission to use the title from, of all people, Visa International, which owned the trademark, something my competitors didn't know. They turned up in high heels and the shortest skirts I had ever seen. Logic prevailed and we won the case. Even though you think you have a good case, you never know what the judge will do on the day.

The next time was more complicated. It started when this salesman turned up who was smarter than any person I had ever met. I thought this guy was an interesting candidate. He was Nigerian and his daddy had sent him to private school in England. He was a charmer. He used to have the script to Wall Street taped to his desk and would make us all cringe as he quoted from the film as he sold ads. He was suave and good-looking and had his fill of girls in the office. He could sell too – he would actually sell at more than the rate card.

He didn't work hard, but he had a very high conversion rate. His only issue was he kept telling people he was from the airline. The airline had enough and asked us to get him off the account. He didn't believe us and started making things difficult for those managing him. We missed what he was doing. He would start conversations and lure people in. For each one he would jot down bits of information.

He was getting ready to sue. He turned up one day dressed like a chauffeur. I asked him what he was doing today, and he replied, "Do you want me to drive you somewhere?" I said "Are you chauffeuring now?" Nothing but idle conversation, but he diarised it. On another day he walked into my office with a tea towel over his arm, and a cup of tea in his hands – I said "What's with the tea towel?" Before I knew it, I was accused of calling him a chauffeur and a waiter. He did this across the business and we ended up in a tribunal for racial harassment.

Luckily for us, the judges didn't believe a word of it. However, we were punished for not curbing the banter in the business. I did have the last laugh, though. He thought he was getting a few thousand dollars payoff – nothing like the £100,000s he had been after – but because he had not paid his rent, his landlords were notified and they took the lot. He ended up with nothing.

The sad part about this was I felt like I had been a surrogate father to him, something he called me on numerous occasions, and had he just stopped the lying he could have been something really special.

The next fight came from a class-action suit in the US, which is a whole different challenge as you can't defend yourself personally there. It was a load of lies, more lies and a few extra lies thrown in for good measure. We finally settled and had to pay off anybody who had worked for us in that year. It was expensive and nearly closed down our US operation.

Not one of the people who got paid off went on to do anything special – it really was tainted money, all those that stayed out of it have gone on and done very well. Just shows you.

One guy, who was making $200,000 a year, got a $30,000 payout. It's been ten years and for the last five of them he's been begging me to take him back, even offering to pay back the money he got as he's never been able to do anything as good since he left. What pissed me off was that he arrived on food stamps and left with a huge house with a swimming pool, yet we had done him wrong in some way.

The only time I took someone to court was recently when a cryptocurrency conman took liberties with us and I remembered why it's a waste of time. We were legally right, we had him bang to rights, yet the judge awarded in his favour – a combination of legal stupidity and probably a better lawyer. I know karma will take over. I looked at their coin and it looks like it's on its last legs. What goes around comes around and I hope he gets the comeuppance he deserves.

When things don't go right, wipe your mouth and move on, use it as a lesson learnt. Sometimes it's an expensive lesson, sometimes you get away cheaply. Life is full of people looking to make a quick buck. As I keep stating throughout the book, you don't stay in business for a very long time behaving in the wrong way. We have been in business for twenty-five years; that's testament to us doing more things right than wrong to people.

Take F'in Action

There isn't a business on Earth that can make every single employee completely happy. Learn from your and their mistakes and move on, otherwise you're taking your eye off the ball. There is nothing more confusing than people. So, if you can't work them out, don't worry – you are not alone.

29

WATCH FROM THE STANDS

ONE OF THE BIGGEST challenges that entrepreneurs, founders, and control-freak bosses like me struggle with, is getting out of the detail, getting off the pitch, and letting their team play.

Over the years, I have managed to delegate more, I have built a great leadership team who I trust to do their job. From time to time, I need to remind them why we are doing this and also refocus them on the task in hand. They might not agree but knowing me, I am more hands-off than I have ever been.

You need to fire yourself from roles, you need to hire people who are better than you at doing what you do. And lose the ego.

One of the most important things you need to do is hire the best coach you can afford. Ideally, someone who has done what you are about to embark upon. At one point, I had three coaches and two personal trainers. I could take on the world.

You need people who will challenge your thinking,

who will ask you difficult questions and hold your feet to the fire. It's easy to pay lip service and carry on with your micromanaging ways. You just will be a small fish in a very big pond.

You need to be watching from the stand enjoying the game and not on the pitch. I still love playing the game and people want to spend time with me, so I started CEO lunches, weekend retreats, and getaways. These gave me a chance to keep connected with the teams while maintaining my focus. This came out of a challenging coaching session.

Over the years, my coaching sessions have taken me to some wonderful places. I have encouraged people to have lunches with me just to spend time talking to them. I would travel around the world if it would get me a one-to-one with the right coach.

It's a very personal thing so you must find someone who is on the right wavelength for you. I saw less of one my great coaches because he said he didn't believe in having any debt and was worried about "what if" situations like I can't get any work and in case of a rainy day. You have to have the confidence in yourself to trade through life. It rains all the time in England. Life is full of what-ifs and if you aren't able to deal with uncertainty, challenge, and fear then you are not the right person for me.

Don't get me wrong, if you don't believe in borrowing money and want a big safety net that's fine but that's not me. If money is cheap, I say borrow it and sweat your assets. We all sit on our assets, accumulating wealth for our retirement and then what happens if we don't make it? That was a great plan. I made sure from the age of forty I would not allow money to get in the way of anything I wanted and have had ten incredible years, and I know it's going to continue. When my number's up, I will not say I wish I did more. I'm living a life to be proud of. I have removed the fears of money, of people, and of business and that has come from great coaching and great training of my brain.

Take F'in Action

Get comfortable with delegating and learn to take a step back. Your team leaders will appreciate the trust and chance to prove themselves and you may find some are even better than you at things.

30

IS FAILING THE BEST WAY TO SUCCEED?

WE FAILED SO MANY TIMES, we failed to deliver in India, Brazil, China, and Russia. However today we still do business in all these markets. We found out the hard way that sometimes doing business in challenging markets is not for the faint-hearted and it's difficult to get money out.

There is a common theme with these territories, you need a good local partner. I think the fact we had so many challenges is probably why we succeeded. You learn when things go wrong, not when things are going swimmingly. No one ever got great in a bull market. It's about knowing when to quit, when to work harder, and more importantly when to go back and learn to be smarter. Good judgement comes from experience and experience – well, that comes from poor judgement. And over the years I made some poor calls, I made some decisions that I wish I could reverse.

Today, the decisions I make are made with a

conscious mind. Then, even if they are not right, I am doing it my way. That way I cannot blame anyone or anything but me. I will make them. There are only a couple of people who I think I made the wrong call on, some I acted too quickly on and others too slowly. When I believed in people, I gave them so many chances. I don't listen to stupid gossip or office politics, it's all such crap. I don't care if people moan about their boss, it's their boss's job to push them to be brilliant; if the relationship is too nice, performance is being sacrificed.

When the world was predicting the end of print, we decided to build a digital business. We chose mobile as the platform. This was the future and we would be the experts in airline apps. No, not the ones that have magazines and media on them but the ones you use to book tickets. They were available in the US and starting in Europe, but Asia and Australia were lagging behind.

We all agreed to spend a couple of hundred thousand on building something. After some months, my partner came back saying he needed a little more money to hire more people and before we knew it, we had ten developers. We had created a small tech company. "It's okay, this was the future," he kept saying. "This will make your shares so valuable." At the same time, I was doing my best to hold the business down and keep the money coming in. He then hired a rock star CTO, who had built super apps; the only problem was this man had no management skills, no hiring skills, and I am convinced didn't really know what he was doing. He was great at making coffee though.

It got out of control very quickly. Bills were arriving from recruitment companies for tens of thousands of pounds and before we knew it, we had blown through millions.

The apps went live on Cebu Pacific in the Philippines and Jetstar in Australia. With hindsight, I think this whole experience messed up our Australian business – at one point we had forty people in Melbourne.

We sold the apps to the airlines, for a nominal sum. They had never paid a penny for these apps, our dream was to build them and then sell ads on them, but by the time they were built no one really wanted to advertise and the airlines were not keen on having too many ads, so the whole process was flawed. You don't need to build the car to drive it, was what we realised from this process. Stick to what you are good at and let others do what they are good at.

At the same time, we had just won five magazines

for American Airlines and Iberia, two huge new contracts. New offices in Miami and Dallas were found and we hired thirty-plus people for these projects, all requiring significant investment.

The incumbents decided to burn bridges and torch the market. Our existing business with other airlines suffered with so much cheap inventory in the marketplace. Putting all of this into the mix created the perfect storm, lots of cash going out with great prospects, but no cash coming in. And then the straw that broke the camel's back – a buyout we could not afford.

Take F'in Action

Listen to what people are saying but also, more importantly, to what's not being said. Always have a detailed plan before starting something big and if things begin to deviate then go back to the plan and review what happened and where things have gone awry.

31

THE BLOT ON THE LANDSCAPE

FAILURE IS AN ACTION not an identity, it's an event not a person. I've talked a little about stress in this book, but stress and pressure have been part of the success of my career and, in the later years, I got really good at dealing with challenges. Make any failure the fuel that drives you. It's a lesson, education, or whatever you want to call it. You must learn from it.

We have overcome so many situations, but our own financial crisis happened in late 2014 and it was a tough moment for me personally. When you work with people for a long time and spend a lot of time in their company you trust them and assume they won't do you wrong. This chapter is me getting some of that frustration off my chest. These are my versions of what happened, and if people see it differently so be it.

Having a good partner is great, you share the burdens, you celebrate the highs and lows, and they help you deal with all the crap you just can't do on your own. I was (and am still) really lucky to have

Michael. For so many years, I have always been grateful for his support and guidance.

It wasn't just us two in 2014, there were four of us. In 2003, Michael and I merged our business with a digital start-up backed by the big venture capitalist 3i. Together, we were four musketeers; somehow, we figured out that airlines were a good business to be in. We all got on well and had very clear roles: Michael oversaw the creative and editorial, I looked after the commercial side, or as I best describe it – I make the money and Michael spends it. (I joke). The other two handled the legal, financial and new business. After eleven years of growing and building together, marriages, divorces, kids, and a couple of failed attempts to sell the business, the cracks began to appear.

The new business guy (the then-CEO) and the accountant could not agree on the way forward. We were caught in the crossfire and always asked to take sides. Board meetings were like a battleground. We went through multiple chairmen as the job of holding everyone on point was becoming too challenging.

Then in November 2013, the two partners decided they could no longer work together. We agreed to pay off the financial partner. Everyone always asks us why we paid him off and to this day I am not sure why. But we did and we live by that decision.

We decided we would go to our bankers to raise money to fund the buyout. We had paid off our previous loan early and the bankers thought this was easy money to lend to us – they did not even do any due diligence. The accountant assured us all that we could afford the loan, he agreed on the terms with the bank and made sure the deal kept on going. In the months leading up to closing the deal, the performance of our US business struggled with the effects of our competitors trouncing the market with cheap pages. And our numbers were under pressure. I remember the accountant asking me, "What do you think we should do?" I said, you need to talk to him and see if he still wants to do the deal. He remained insistent that we could afford the loan.

The accountants advised that the company had collected in monies but had slowed down paying people. Yes, our cash position looked good – yet, all was not as it seemed. The night before the deal, the other partner came to me and asked how I was feeling. I said I feel good for the long-term prospects of the business if, in the short-term, it looked a little tough. I said renegotiate the price, or postpone for a bit, we don't have to do the deal. He said it was ungentlemanly to renege on the price. I told him then that was the most stupid thing to say. It's a deal, the situation has changed. That's life. Michael re-invested at this point and I actually took some money out, as I had a personal issue that I had to fund, which, at the time, was a real headache. But it turned out to be a godsend. As I said earlier, your problems are sometimes the solution.

He was adamant and the deal went ahead. Champagne dinners followed, everyone was happy, the CEO had a huge stake in the business. He was delighted. Then we came to our first test, ninety days in and the shit hit the fan. We missed our covenant and the bank went into meltdown, what ensued was just stupid panic from the bank. We hadn't missed a payment, yet they put us in the bad boys' club and a young lad was given the job of dealing with our account. After all, we had £50m in turnover and were profitable. He was out of his depth and before we knew it, he had brought in one of the big accountancy firms.

The bills were racking up fast and, if it wasn't enough, we were short of cash. The bank was making us pay hundreds of thousands of pounds in fees which we clearly could not afford. Add in legal fees and forensic accountants and the cash was running out, while the bank was spending for fun. This is an issue that small and medium sized businesses struggle with when they come under pressure from their lenders. It needs addressing.

When you have a young person from a big accountancy firm telling you that you need to switch off the lights on a business that you have worked hard to build and given every inch of your being for for twenty years, that's when the fighter in you comes out. She and her colleagues told the bank that we were incapable of rescuing the business, and that it was not salvageable. She and all her partners were not correct, and I am so glad I had the chance to prove them so embarrassingly wrong. We are here and stronger than ever.

What was worse was that the accountant had an opportunity to save us, and instead, he acted in a very selfish manner and tried to manipulate the situation to make a huge personal gain – it was pure greed. We were left to fight the bankers alone. What happened next was nothing more than instinct. With no experience in dealing with bankers, accountants, and expensive lawyers, I went to battle, as I refused to let these people close down the business we had spent twenty years building. We removed the other partner, he'd caused most of the frustration, wasting millions on a digital dream, hiring the wrong people, and not having the balls to stand up to the banks.

There is not a week goes by where I wish things had turned out differently. He was a nice guy but had lost the plot. He was Ivy League educated and the accountant had gone to Eton, and here was little old me, fighting the lot of them.

At 5:30 pm on a Friday night, the bank emailed us that they had sold our debt. They kept ignoring my calls and emails and it was midnight before I got hold of anyone. I got them to agree to give me to lunchtime on Monday to raise the money, which I did. It was a frantic weekend, sadly the deal didn't materialise the way we had planned, but I managed to keep buying more time until we were able to bring in new investors and save the business. Those six months up to early March 2015 were the most horrific of my professional career. It's also where I learned the most about myself and about what I was capable of doing. The thought of telling three hundred people they were out of work and twenty airlines they would have no magazines this month was a real motivator.

During the whole process, I was actually very calm and considered. I didn't feel panic, I'm not sure why. I operated with clarity and precision, I found solace in a few friends who gave me sensible advice. I was clear in what outcome I wanted. I just wish I had negotiated a better deal at the time with the new investors. They did take advantage of our weak position, but that's their line of work.

At the time, no one in the company knew what was going on; we had only told a few people who helped us while we went about saving the business. To the whole company, it was business as normal. Michael and I went about renegotiating deals with airlines, resigning work that didn't make sense anymore and focusing on what we were good at – selling advertisements and producing great content. Closing our Australian operation was one of the first things we did, which was a bloody shame, as I loved the country and spending time down under.

Within a year, the business was back in profit and over the next three years we doubled profits every year. We stuck to what we were good at, we focused on every part of the business, and with Michael and me back in charge, the results were sensational. We also managed to find a new investor and deliver a very healthy return for our partners who had bailed us out. So much so, they took us on a fantastic day out by private jet to say thank you – lunch in San Sebastian, Spain, at a Michelin-starred restaurant, which inspired an incentive for my sales team.

I learnt a lot about myself during this period. I learnt that despite always joking I was worried people would find out I had no idea what I was doing. I clearly did and was a capable operator. Since that day, I have never been so confident in my ability, nothing phases me or scares me and I believe that the Lucky Leslie journey continues. So much so I bought a horse and called it Lucky Leslie and it will run later this year. I can't wait to see him win.

With hindsight, the whole process gave me the confidence to be a better leader. To put people's interests ahead of mine. It made me realise that I was capable of much more than I had achieved so far. I was determined to show the world that Ink was destined to be a name associated with brilliant sales, amazing content and a company that shaped travel media as we consume it today and for the years to come.

Take F'in Action

If you decide to take on a business partner then outline your individual responsibilities, strengths, and weaknesses in the beginning. Make sure you are compatible and really challenge each other.

32

LETTER TO SALES PEOPLE EVERYWHERE

Dear Seller,

Whatever you decide to do in life, be proud of yourself. Find something that you are prepared to put the hard yards into.

You must work out what and who you need around you to achieve it. There is no easy route, no life hack to success, so stop looking for shortcuts. It takes so many hours to be good at anything. I have been at this sales game for over 70,000 hours and I have not yet achieved mastery. I'm learning new stuff every single day, that proves you can never know enough about your craft.

Be proud of being a salesperson, sales is a noble art. And being good at it is akin to any other skill. The craft improves with age and experience and you never stop learning. And if anyone tells you that sales is not a proper job, remind them that nothing in life happens until someone sells something.

Your thoughts will either create space or tension. Just knowing this can help you to deal with life more easily. Create more space, spend more time thinking positively and finding solutions. Don't waste time and energy dwelling on things you can't change.

Have no regrets, make decisions consciously and don't do anything you don't want to do. Say "NO" often and be confident that your time is better spent elsewhere. Life is full of people who think they know it all, but there are very few people who know that much. Everyone has problems. Don't ever wish for things to be easier, just make sure you find a way to be stronger. No one has a perfect life and anyone you think has it all, definitely doesn't.

Few things in life are certain. You know on what day you were born. We have no idea how many days are available to us from that day. Just make as many of them winning days and life will turn out more than fine. Never forget to tell people that you love them, always say thank you, and really appreciate every day you get. Any day above the ground is good. Life is too short to mope around and don't dwell on the shit, 'cos shit happens!

And finally, make sure you are adding value to everyone you meet. Help enough people get what they want and your life will be truly magical.

Take F'in Action

If your day is not going well then do something that makes you feel happy and/or loved. See a friend. Watch a good film. Do something for someone else. Work out the steps involved to achieve what you want. You need to realise you might not get what you want and you certainly won't always get appreciation for working hard. Understand that your greatest fears are actually your greatest strengths. What's really scary is not living. The more you do, the better you get at it.

33

FINAL THOUGHTS

TODAY I DESCRIBE myself as an alchemist. I look to create magic in every situation, I don't care what the logical answer is. Most companies will not fire anyone for thinking logically, I think differently. I want to challenge the status quo and do things that will get us the greatest results. There are still some things that have eluded me, and knowing that I have been truly successful is definitely one of them.

I'm on a flight to Miami, a route I've done countless times, more recently enjoying the comfort at the front of the plane. I scrutinize my appearance in the small, square mirror in the bathroom. My reflection looks back at me, challenging my thoughts.

I still question my success. I have made money for myself, investors, and many others. I have made my people much more successful than some of them ever imagined they could be. But I am still missing the metric that says you have done good rather than been just lucky. That's something I still need to figure out.

Success is such a personal benchmark and yet I still struggle to see myself as successful. I have had so many magic moments and memories to savour.

I know I am certainly more capable than I give myself credit for. I am great at spotting talent, I am good at giving people a cause to believe in and a leader to trust. I'm an excellent judge of character, most of the time. Through my ability to tell stories, I can change people's state of mind. I've learnt to be more patient and sympathetic as I've aged. I've even improved my empathy, though my eleven-year-old says I still have a lot of work to do. I continue to learn and improve.

I still make excuses about my weight, (so much so that *There is No F in Weight Loss* will come next, followed by *There is No F in Leadership*) and I was too quick to make jokes at mine and other people's expense. Over the years, I've also learned I really like people – I enjoy talking and, more importantly, listening. It's something I've improved in as I've gotten older.

Sometimes I attempted to fix too many things, too quickly, and I've now realised that many problems people have don't have a quick fix. Rather, that person needs to figure it out for themselves. I still try, though: I could come along and say exactly the same message as one of my colleagues and yet somehow I would get through to them. In the early days, this frustrated my team, later on, they would use it sensibly. They call it magic dust.

I've created a wonderful life for myself through sheer determination to help others get better and that is the overriding message I want to leave you with. Life is shorter than most of us want and if you don't make each day count you are just wasting time. Make sure you are invested in whatever it is you do, not just interested. The investment you put into it affects the returns you get out of it.

Be the best you can; it's not a crowded market place. No matter what you decide to sell, make sure you have passion for the product, make sure someone will pay you for it, do something you are good at, and ensure it is something the world needs. If you can tick all of these boxes, you will be very successful.

Finally, I have come to the conclusion that no matter what you crave out of life – happiness, success or peace of mind – they all revolve around relationships and how good they are. It's key to getting the most out of life. Surround yourself with the right people and build the strongest forms of friendships, and not with people who just agree with you. If you do this, life will continue to improve.

Conversely, you should breakaway from the ones who are weak or add little value to your life and demand time with those who you want to be like or learn from. And I mean demand. Every time you find a challenge, it's normally linked to a breakdown in a relationship somewhere. The best relationships are frequently turbulent, and that's healthy too – don't be the person who is everyone's fixer, or everyone's shoulder to cry on. Be the creative one who inspires and motivates – that's the sales hero.

As I noted earlier, do feel free to connect with me online or reach out via email if you have any questions about my story or if you feel I could help you.

There is a lot of valuable information in this book and it's always great to share. Particularly, if you are the kind of person who will use the advice in these pages to take action to improve yourself and your career. Often, we need someone to stay accountable to and a great way to do this is by recommending this book to someone so you can take action together.

I'll finish this exactly as every email I ever send to my sales team.

SELL WELL.

Printed in Great
Britain
by Amazon

31059937R00115